英語で読む
アンデルセン名作選
The Best of Andersen's Fairy Tales

ハンス・クリスチャン・アンデルセン
原作

谷口幸夫
英語解説

佐藤和枝
翻訳

カバーイラスト
Arthur Edmund Dulac, 1837, Wikipedia
•
英文リライト
David Olivier
•
ナレーション
Lindsay Nelson, Carolyn Miller

本書の英語テキストは、弊社から刊行された
ラダーシリーズ『The Best of Andersen's Fairy Tales　アンデルセン名作選』から転載しています。

はじめに

　ハンス・クリスチャン・アンデルセン（以下、アンデルセン）の作品を思いつくまま挙げてみよう。『赤い靴』『親指姫』『人魚姫』『裸の王さま』『マッチ売りの少女』『みにくいアヒルの子』『雪の女王』などなど。おそらく幼少の頃、布団の中で、何度もよみきかせしてもらった童話ばかりであろう。最近では、『アナと雪の女王（*Frozen*）』のように、ディズニー映画の大ヒット作品にもアンデルセンの原作が使われることも少なくない。

　さて、アンデルセンとはどんな人物なのだろうか。Wikipediaには、次のような記載がなされている。

＊　＊　＊

　ハンス・クリスチャン・アンデルセン（Hans Christian Andersen）、1805年4月2日-1875年8月4日）は、デンマークの代表的な童話作家、詩人である。デンマークでは、Andersenが非常にありふれた姓であることから、フルネームを略したH. C. Andersen（デンマーク語読みで"ホー・セー・アナスン"）と呼ばれる。

　アンデルセンは、両親の強い愛と、母親の盲信によって、想像力豊かな「天才児」として育っていく。しかし、天才と称賛されて育ったところから、挫折に次ぐ挫折を経たことから、かなりいびつな性格の人物だったらしい。

　厭世家なのだが、欧州遍歴の経験もあって知人・友人は大変に多く、人間への観察力は作品を通してかなり鋭いものだったことが伺える。

　若い頃は苦境に次ぐ苦境だったこともあり、「人間は死ぬ以外に幸せになる方法などない」というかなり尖った哲学を持った作品が多く、初期の童話はその色の濃さから当初は不興を買うほどだった。これは同時に「そ

んな幸せしかない」貧困層の悲痛な叫びに、社会が見て見ぬふりをする状況を批判したものともいわれる。

　極度の心配性でもあり、旅先には必ずロープを携帯し、非常時に脱出できるよう備えていた。

　また晩年には、「生きているのに埋葬されかけた男の話」を聞き、それ以来自分の枕元に「まだ死んでいません」とわざわざメモを置いて寝ていたという。

＊　＊　＊

　アンデルセンの童話のあらすじは、だいたい頭の中に入っているので、本書を読んでいくと、頭の中に英文がたまりやすくなっていると言える。特に付属のCDと一緒に音読すると、よりいっそう英語が頭の中に残る。

　4つの話の冒頭の英文を、ぜひ暗唱してみるといいだろう。皆さんも、日本昔話の「むかしむかし、あるところに…」まで聞けば、老若男女を問わず、ほとんどの人が「おじいさんとおばあさんが住んでいました」と何も見ないでも、暗唱することができるはず。これは、『桃太郎』を幼少期に何度も何度も繰り返し聞いたおかげで、頭の脳の中にすり込まれているのだ。言ってみれば、「身体の一部」と言えよう。

　英語学習の観点から言えば、暗唱できるぐらいまで音読することを目標にしてほしい。全文は無理だろうから、最初の一文だけでもいいだろう。最初の『人魚姫』、次の『裸の王さま』、そして『すずの兵隊』、さらには『みにくいアヒルの子』の4つの話の最初の一文をマスターしてみよう。そこから本格的な英語学習がはじまるかもしれない。

　小さな成功が、きっと後々大きな感動を呼び起こしてくれますよ。

谷口　幸夫

CONTENTS

The Little Mermaid 7
人魚姫

The Emperor's New Clothes 93
裸の王さま

The Steadfast Tin Soldier 115
すずの兵隊

The Ugly Duckling 137
みにくいアヒルの子

本書の構成

本書は、

- □ 英日対訳による本文
- □ 覚えておきたい英語表現
- □ 欄外の語注
- □ MP3形式の英文音声

で構成されています。

本書は、「アンデルセン童話」をやさしい英語で書きあらためた本文に、日本語訳をつけました。

各ページの下部には、英語を読み進める上で助けとなるよう単語・熟語の意味が掲載されています。また左右ページは、段落のはじまりが対応していますので、日本語を読んで英語を確認するという読み方もスムーズにできるようになっています。またストーリーごとに英語解説がありますので、本文を楽しんだ後に、英語の使い方などをチェックしていただくのに最適です。

付属のCD-ROMについて

本書に付属のCD-ROMに収録されている音声は、パソコンや携帯音楽プレーヤーなどで再生することができるMP3ファイル形式です。一般的な音楽CDプレーヤーでは再生できませんので、ご注意ください。

■音声ファイルについて

付属のCD-ROMには、本書の英語パートの朗読音声が収録されています。本文左ページに出てくるヘッドホンマーク内の数字とファイル名の数字がそれぞれ対応しています。

パソコンや携帯プレーヤーで、お好きな箇所を繰り返し聴いていただくことで、発音のチェックだけでなく、英語で物語を理解する力が自然に身に付きます。

■音声ファイルの利用方法について

CD-ROMをパソコンのCD/DVDドライブに入れて、iTunesなどの音楽再生（管理）ソフトにCD-ROM上の音声ファイルを取り込んでご利用ください。

■パソコンの音楽再生ソフトへの取り込みについて

パソコンにMP3形式の音声ファイルを再生できるアプリケーションがインストールされていることをご確認ください。

通常のオーディオCDと異なり、CD-ROMをパソコンのCD/DVDドライブに入れても、多くの場合音楽再生ソフトは自動的に起動しません。ご自分でアプリケーションを直接起動して、「ファイル」メニューから「ライブラリに追加」したり、再生ソフトのウインドウ上にファイルをマウスでドラッグ＆ドロップするなどして取り込んでください。

音楽再生ソフトの詳しい操作方法や、携帯音楽プレーヤーへのファイルの転送方法については、ソフトやプレーヤーに付属のマニュアルやオンラインヘルプで確認するか、アプリケーションの開発元にお問い合わせください。

The Little Mermaid

人魚姫

The Little Mermaid

Far out at sea the water is as blue as the loveliest blueflower and as clear as glass. But it is very deep— deeper than man can reach and deeper than many tall churches, one upon the other. Down there live people called the Sea-folk.

Please don't think that there is only white sand at the sea bottom. No, indeed! The most wonderful trees and plants grow there. Just a little movement of the water moves the leaves back and forth. The plants really look alive. And all the fish, big and small, swim among the branches just as the birds fly about the trees up here. In the deepest spot of all lies the Sea-King's palace. The walls and windows are made of beautiful sea plants and the tops of shells. These shells are lovely. In every one there lies a large, shining pearl.

■reach 動（目的地に）達する　■church 名教会　■one upon the other 積み重ねる　■folk 名人々　■indeed 副確かに、いかにも　■plant 名植物　■branch 名枝　■fly about 飛び回る　■lie 動ある、置かれてある　■palace 名宮殿

人魚姫

　海のはるか沖では、水の色は、もっとも美しいブルーフラワーより青く、ガラスと同じくらいすきとおっています。けれども、海はとても深いのです。人間が底まで行きつけるよりも、そして、たくさんの高い教会を次から次へと積み重ねたよりも深いのです。海の底には、人魚と呼ばれる一族が住んでいます。

　海底には白い砂しかない、とは思わないでください。いいえ、そんなことはありません！　そこには、最高にすばらしい木や植物が生えているのです。水がほんのわずかに動いただけでも、葉っぱは前後に揺れます。植物は本当に生き生きとしています。そして、魚はみんな、大きいのも小さいのも、枝の間を泳いでいます。それはまるで地上の鳥が枝の間を飛びまわるようです。海底のもっとも深いところに、人魚の王の宮殿があります。壁や窓は、美しい海の植物や貝がらでできています。とてもきれいな貝がらです。どの貝がらの中にも、大きな輝く真珠が入っています。

The Little Mermaid

The Sea-King's wife had died many years ago, so his aged mother took care of his house. She was a wise woman. She was also proud of the family she was born into. She was an important person among the Sea-folk, so she wore twelve oysters on her tail. The other important folk could only wear six. Most folk thought highly of her; especially because she took loving care of the little Sea-princesses, her granddaughters. They were six pretty girls, but the youngest one was the loveliest of them all. Her skin was the color of a rose leaf, and her eyes were as blue as the deepest sea. But, like the others, she had no feet. Her body ended in a fish's tail.

All day long they used to play in the palace's great rooms. There, the living flowers grew upon the walls. When the tall windows were opened, the fish would swim in; just as birds fly into our homes when we open the windows. The fish would swim up to the little princesses and eat from their hands.

■aged 形年老いた　■take care of ～を世話する　■be proud of ～を誇りに思う　■oyster 名カキ　■think highly of ～を尊敬する　■used to かつてはよく～したものだ　■living 形生きている　■just as ～と同じように　■up to ～まで(に)

人魚姫

　人魚の王のお妃さまは何年も前に死んでしまったので、王さまの年をとったお母さまが家の面倒を見ていました。お母さまはかしこい方でした。また、彼女は自分の家柄を誇りに思っていました。おばあさまは人魚の中で重要な地位にあったので、しっぽに12個のカキをつけていました。他の重要な人々は、六個しかつけられませんでした。人魚の多くは、おばあさまを尊敬していました。特に尊敬に値したのは、おばあさまが孫娘である小さな人魚姫たちの世話を愛情いっぱいにしていたからです。六人の人魚姫はみんなきれいでしたが、一番末の姫が一番美しいのでした。その肌はバラの葉っぱの色で、目は一番深い海と同じくらい青いのでした。けれども、他の人魚と同じく、彼女には足がありませんでした。体の先の方は魚のしっぽでした。

　一日中、お姫さまたちは宮殿の大きな部屋で遊んでいたものでした。そこには、壁の上に、生きた花が生えていました。大きな窓が開いていると、魚が泳いで入ってきました。まるで私たちの家で窓を開けた時に鳥が飛び込んでくるような様子でした。魚は小さな人魚のお姫さまたちのそばまで泳いできて、手からエサを食べました。

The Little Mermaid

Around the palace was a large garden full of bright red and dark blue trees; the fruit shined like gold, and the flowers like burning fire. The soil itself was the finest blue sand. Everything had a bluish color. One might think that one was up in the sky rather than at the bottom of the sea. And when the sea was still, one could see the sun; it looked like a bright, red flower.

Each of the little princesses had her own garden where she could plant as she pleased. One princess gave her flower-place the form of a large fish; another the form of a mermaid. But the youngest planted hers in a circle to look like the sun. She used only the reddest of flowers. She was an unusual child, quiet and thoughtful. Her sisters liked to fill their gardens with strange things from sunken ships. But, beside her sunny flowers, she had only a pretty statue of a handsome boy. It was made of white marble which she found on a sunken ship. Next to this statue she planted a tree with long leaves. It is called a willow tree. The willow's leaves waved back and forth nearly touching the soil.

■soil 名（表層の）土　■bluish 形青みがかった　■still 形静かな　■unusual 形他とは異なる　■sunken 形沈没した　■beside 前〜の傍らに　■statue 名像　■marble 名大理石　■willow 名ヤナギ

人魚姫

　宮殿のまわりには、鮮やかな赤色と濃い青色の木がたくさん生えている大きなお庭がありました。木の実は金のように輝き、花は燃える炎のような色でした。地面そのものは、とても細かい青い砂でした。すべてのものが青っぽい色でしたので、海底にいるというよりも、まるで空に浮かんでいるのかと錯覚しそうでした。海が穏やかな時は、太陽を見ることができました。それは、鮮やかな赤い花のように見えました。

　小さな人魚のお姫さまたちは、それぞれ自分の庭をもっており、そこに自分が好きなものを植えることができました。あるお姫さまは庭を大きな魚の形にしました。他のお姫さまは、人魚の形にしました。でも、一番末のお姫さまは、庭を太陽のような丸い形にしました。彼女はもっとも赤い花しか植えませんでした。このお姫さまは普通の子とちがい、静かで思慮深い子どもでした。お姉さまたちは、自分の庭を、沈没船からもってきた不思議なもので飾っていました。けれども末のお姫さまは、お日さまのような花のほかには、ハンサムな男の子の美しい像だけを飾っていました。その像は白い大理石でできており、彼女はそれを沈んだ船で見つけたのでした。その像のとなりに、彼女は長い葉のついた木を植えました。それはヤナギという木で、その葉は前後に揺れて、地面に触れそうでした。

The Little Mermaid

Her greatest joy was to hear about the world of mankind above. She made her old grandmother tell her about ships and towns, people and animals. She thought it was especially wonderful that the flowers on earth could be smelled; they cannot be smelled at the bottom of the sea. Also, that the woods were green and that the fishes in the branches could sing loudly and beautifully. It was the birds, you see, that her grandmother called fishes. Her granddaughters had never seen birds, and, therefore, couldn't understand.

"When you reach your fifteenth birthday," said the grandmother, "you may rise up out of the sea. You may sit in the moonshine on the rocks and see the big ships sail by. Forests and cities you shall also see."

In the following year, the oldest sister would become fifteen; but how about the others? Each girl was one year younger than the next, so the youngest would have to wait five whole years. Then she too could come up and see what our world is like. But each sister promised to tell the others what she saw and what she enjoyed the most. There were many things their grandmother did not tell them which they wanted to know.

■joy 名喜び(の種)　■mankind 名人間　■have never seen 見たことがない　■therefore 副それゆえに　■may 助～してもよろしい　■rise 動(高い場所に)上がる　■sail 動帆走する

人魚姫

　彼女が一番楽しみにしていたのは、海の上にある人間の世界について聞くことでした。おばあさまにせがんで、船や町、人々や動物について話してもらいました。彼女がもっともすばらしいと思ったのは、地上の花には香りがあるということでした。海底の花には香りがないのです。また、森は緑で、枝にいる魚は、大きく美しい声で歌うことができるというのです。もちろん、これは鳥のことでしたが、おばあさまは魚と呼んだのでした。孫娘たちは鳥を見たことがなかったので、鳥と言ってもわからなかったでしょう。

　「おまえたちが15歳になったら」と、おばあさまは言いました。「上へ泳いでいって、海の外へ出てもいいですよ。月明かりのもとで、岩の上に座り、大きな船が通り過ぎていくのを見たり、森や町を見たりできるのです」
　次の年には、一番上のお姉さまが15歳になるはずでした。他の娘たちはというと、それぞれ一歳ずつ離れていたので、一番下のお姫さまは5年も待たなければなりませんでした。その時になってやっと彼女も上へ泳いでいって、世界がどのようなものかを見ることができるのです。けれども、姉妹たちはそれぞれ、自分が見たことと、何が一番楽しかったかを他の姉妹に話す、ということを約束しました。彼女たちが知りたいのに、おばあさまは話してくれなかったことがたくさんありました。

The Little Mermaid

But it was the youngest girl who wanted to know more than the others. She also had the longest time to wait. Often she stood at the open window and looked up through the dark blue water. Beyond the swimming fish she could see the moon and stars. They were not so bright, of course, but they were there. When something like a dark cloud passed overhead, she knew it was either a large fish or a ship with many people. Certainly the people on board the ship never dreamed that a pretty mermaid stood below looking up at them.

And now the oldest princess was fifteen years old and able to rise to the surface of the sea. When she came back she had hundreds of things to tell her sisters. But the nicest thing of all, she said, was to lie in the moonshine on a sandbank. From there by the shore she could see the large town and its many lights. The lights looked like stars. She could also hear the noises of busy people and of bells ringing in their churches. She had a strong desire to go on shore. But she knew she could not.

■overhead 副 頭上に　■either A or B AかそれともB　■certainly 副 確かに　■on board a ship 船上で　■surface 名 水面　■sandbank 名（河口などの）砂州　■shore 名 岸　■desire 名 願望、欲望

人魚姫

　けれども、ほかのお姫さまたちのだれよりも、いろいろなことを知りたかったのは、一番若いお姫さまでした。それなのに、彼女は一番長い間、待たなければなりませんでした。彼女はしばしば開いた窓の前に立ち、深い青色の水を通して上を見上げていました。泳いでいる魚の間に、彼女は月や星を見ることができました。それは、もちろんそれほど明るく見えませんでしたが、それでも、そこにあることはわかりました。暗い雲のようなものが上を通り過ぎた時には、それは大きな魚か、たくさんの人間が乗っている船だということを彼女は知っていました。もちろん、その船に乗っている人々は、まさか海底に美しい人魚が立っていて自分たちを見上げているなどとは、夢にも思いませんでした。

　さて、いよいよ一番上のお姫さまは15歳になり、海の上へと泳いでいけることになりました。彼女がもどってきた時には、妹たちに話したいことが山ほどありました。しかし、彼女が一番すばらしいと思ったのは、月光をあびながら浅瀬に横たわっていることだった、と言いました。岸の近くのその場所から、彼女は大きな町と、たくさんの光を見ました。その光は、まるで星のようでした。彼女はまた、人々が忙しく動きまわっている音や、教会のベルが鳴る音を聞くことができました。陸地に行ってみたい、と強く思いましたが、それはできないことだとわかっていました。

The Little Mermaid

Oh, how the younger sister listened! And afterwards, she stood in the evening at the open window. She looked up through the water and thought of the great city with all its people and noise. She even thought she heard the church bells ringing.

The next year the second sister was allowed to rise to the surface. She too could swim anywhere she wanted. She went up just as the sun was going down. And she thought the sunset was the prettiest sight of all. The whole sky looked like gold, she said; and the beauty of the clouds was beyond words. Red, orange and pink, they sailed over her head. But faster than the clouds was a group of wild ducks flying in front of the sun. She also swam towards the sun, but it sank into the sea before she could get to it.

■afterwards 副その後　■allow 動許可する　■sunset 名日没　■sight 名景色　■beyond 前〜を凌駕する　■wild duck 野生のカモ　■sank 動sink（沈む）の過去形　■get to 〜に達する

人魚姫

　ああ、一番下のお姫さまは、どんなに熱心にお姉さまの話を聞いたことでしょう！　そのあと、彼女は夜に、開いた窓の前に立っていました。水を通して上を見上げ、たくさんの人々が住み、いろいろな音がしている大きな町のことを考えました。教会の鐘が鳴るのが聞こえたような気がするほどでした。

　次の年、上から二番目のお姉さまが、水面へ泳いでいくことを許されました。自分が行きたいところならどこへでも、泳いでいくことができたのです。彼女が水上に出た時は、太陽がまさに沈もうとしている時でした。彼女は、日没が一番美しい景色だと思いました。このお姉さまが言うには、空全体が金色に輝いていたそうです。そして雲の美しいことといったら、言葉にたとえようもありませんでした。赤、オレンジそしてピンク色の雲が、彼女の頭の上を通り過ぎていきました。その雲よりも早く、野生のカモたちが太陽の前を飛んでいきました。彼女も太陽に向かって泳いでいきましたが、太陽は彼女がたどり着く前に海に沈んでしまいました。

The Little Mermaid

A year after that the third sister came up to the surface. She had no fear, so she swam up a broad river from the sea. She saw pretty green hills covered with fruit trees; castles and country houses hidden by the lovely woods; she heard the birds singing; and the bright sun made her face burn. In a small stream she came across lots of children. They were running around with no clothes and playing in the water. She wanted to play with them. But when they saw her they became afraid and ran away. Soon, a little black animal began shouting at her. It was a dog, but she had never seen a dog before. Then she became afraid and swam back to the open sea. But never could she forget the lovely woods, the green hills and the pretty children—the children who could swim in the water without fish tails.

The fourth sister did not go near the shore. Instead, she stayed out in the middle of the sea and said that was the nicest of all. One could see for miles and miles around, and the sky looked like a large glass bell. She had seen ships too, but far away. She saw fish called dolphins, which could jump high into the air. And the largest creatures in the sea, called whales, blew water up through their noses.

■fear 名恐れ　■broad 形（幅が）広い　■hill 名丘　■burn 動熱くなる　■stream 名小川、細流　■run around 走り回る　■stay out 外にいる　■creature 名生き物

人魚姫

　それから一年して、三番目のお姉さまが水面へと泳いでいきました。彼女はおそれを知らない娘だったので、海から広い川の上流へ泳いでいきました。果物の木が生えている美しい緑の丘、すばらしい森の陰に隠れている宮殿や家々が見えました。鳥のさえずりが聞こえました。そして、太陽の光があまりにもまぶしくて、顔が熱くなるほどでした。細い流れにさしかかると、子どもがたくさんいました。彼らは裸で走りまわり、水の中で遊んでいました。彼女は子どもたちと遊びたかったのですが、子どもたちは彼女を見ると、怖がって逃げていってしまいました。すぐに、小さな黒い動物が彼女に向かって吠え始めました。それは犬でした。彼女は犬を見たことがなかったので怖くなり、海へもどりました。けれども、彼女はあの美しい森、緑の丘、そして魚のしっぽがないのに水の中で泳ぐことができる、あのかわいい子どもたちのことを、けっして忘れることはできませんでした。

　上から四番目のお姉さまは、岸の近くまでは行きませんでした。そのかわりに、彼女は海のまん中にただよい、それが一番すてきなことだったと言いました。何マイルも先の方まで見渡すことができて、空は大きなガラスの鐘のようでした。彼女も船を何そうか見かけましたが、それは遠くの方にありました。イルカという魚も見ました。それは空高く飛び上がることができるのでした。そしてクジラと呼ばれる、海に住んでいる中で一番大きな生き物が、鼻から水を噴き上げているのも見ました。

The Little Mermaid

Then it was the turn of the fifth sister. Her birthday was in the winter. She saw what the others had not seen their first times. The sea had quite a green color with very large, white ice mountains floating about. Each looked like a pearl, she said. They had the strangest forms and shone like diamonds. She sat on one of the largest ice mountains and watched the ships pass by. The ships all seemed very afraid of the ice. In the evening, the sky became cloudy and stormy. She enjoyed the wind blowing her long hair. All the ships took down their sails. She could see the fear in the sailors' eyes as they passed near the giant ice mountain. Yet she sat quietly in the middle of the troubled sea.

The first time each of the sisters rose to the surface was always a new and wondrous experience. All of them were surprised by the beautiful things they saw. Later, however, when they could go above anytime they wanted, they were no longer very interested. After that first time, they didn't care so much about the world above. They longed to stay in the deep water. It was nicest down below at home, they said.

■turn 名順番　■float about 辺りを漂う　■pass by 通り掛かる　■stormy 形嵐の
■take down 降ろす　■sail 名帆　■wondrous 形驚くべき　■however 副けれども
■long to ～することを切望する

人魚姫

　その次は、上から五番目のお姉さまの番でした。彼女の誕生日は冬だったので、他のお姫さまたちが初めて行った時には見えなかったものを見ました。海は深い緑色で、とても大きな白い氷の山々が浮かんでいました。それはみんな、まるで真珠のようだった、と彼女は言いました。それらはとても不思議な形をしていて、ダイヤモンドのように輝いていました。彼女は大きな氷の山の上に座り、いろいろな船が通り過ぎていくのを見ていました。どの船も、氷をとてもおそれているように見えました。夜になると空が曇ってきて、嵐になりました。彼女は自分の長い髪が風に吹かれているのを楽しみました。すべての船は帆をたたんでいました。船が巨大な氷の山のそばを通り過ぎていく時、船員たちの目に恐怖が宿っているのが見えました。それでも彼女は荒れた海のまん中に、静かに座っていました。

　海の上へ泳いでいったお姉さまたちにとって、最初の時はすべてが新しく、驚きに満ちた経験でした。みんな自分たちが見た美しいものに驚きました。けれども、その後、いつでも海面に上っていってもよいようになると、彼女たちはあまり上の世界に興味をもたなくなりました。一度経験してしまったあとは、彼女たちは水上の世界のことをあまり気にかけなくなったのです。それよりも、深い海にとどまっていたいのでした。彼女たちは、この海の中の自分たちの家が一番よいと言うのでした。

The Little Mermaid

Often in the evenings the five sisters would hold hands and rise in a row to the water's surface. All of them had beautiful voices, sweeter than any human's. When a storm was blowing and they thought a ship might sink, they would swim in front of the ship. Then they would sing sweetly to the sailors. They told the sailors of the beautiful world under the sea, and not to be afraid to come down. But the sailors couldn't understand their words. They thought the voices came from the wind. Nor did the sailors ever see the beautiful Sea-King's palace; for the men were always dead when their bodies reached the sea bottom.

Now when the sisters rose together to the surface, the little sister would stand and watch them from the window. She felt sad and alone and wanted to cry. But mermaids have no tears and so they suffer even more.

"Oh, I wish I were fifteen!" said she. "I know that I shall love the world above and the men who live there."

And at last she became fifteen years old.

■nor 接 ～もまた…ない ■ever 副 かつて ■suffer 動 苦しむ ■even more さらにいっそう ■I wish I were ～だったらよかったのに ■shall 助 ～するつもりである ■at last とうとう

人魚姫

　夕方になると、しばしば五人の姉妹は手をとりあって、一列になり、水面まで上っていきました。彼女たちはみな、どのような人間よりも甘い、美しい声の持ち主でした。嵐が吹き荒れて船が沈みそうだと思った時は、彼女たちは船の前に泳いで行き、そして船乗りたちに甘く歌いかけるのでした。海の中には美しい世界があるので、沈んでも怖がることはないのです、と話しかけていたのです。けれども、船乗りたちにはお姫さまたちの言葉がわからなかったので、その声を風の音だと思いました。人魚の王の美しい宮殿を見たことがある船乗りもいませんでした。人間の体が海底に沈んだ時には、彼らはすでに死んでいたからです。

　お姉さまたちがみんないっしょに水面へ上っていく時には、末の妹は立ったまま、彼女たちを窓から見ていました。悲しくて、寂しくて、泣きたくなりました。けれども、人魚には涙というものがないので、いっそう苦しいのです。
　「ああ、私が15歳ならよいのに！」と彼女は言いました。「私だったら上の世界と、そこに住む人々を愛するでしょうに」
　そしてとうとう、末のお姫さまも15歳になりました。

The Little Mermaid

"Well, now we don't have to worry about you anymore," said her grandmother. "Come here and let me dress you like your sisters." And she placed a hat of white sea flowers in her hair. Then the old lady tied eight large oysters to the Princess' tail. Everyone would know she was an important mermaid.

"But they hurt me so!" said the little mermaid.

"Yes, but sometimes we must suffer for the right appearances," said her grandmother.

Oh, how glad the little mermaid would have been not to wear these fine things. She liked the red flowers from her garden much better. But she didn't dare take them off. "Goodbye!" she said and rose lightly up to the surface.

The sun had just set when she raised her head above the water. The clouds were pink and gold. In the middle of the sky shined the evening star, clear and lovely. The air was cool and fair, the sea like glass.

■hurt 動 〜に苦痛を与える　■appearance 名 外観　■would have been 〜だとしたら　■fine 形 立派な　■dare 動 〜する勇気がある　■take 〜 off 〜を外す　■fair 形 清らかな

人魚姫

「やれやれ、私たちはもうおまえのことを心配しなくてもよいのですね」と、おばあさまが言いました。「ここにいらっしゃい。おまえをお姉さまたちと同じように身づくろいしてあげるから」そして、彼女は白い海の花でできた帽子を、お姫さまの髪に乗せました。それからおばあさまは、お姫さまのしっぽに八つの大きなカキを結びつけました。これで、お姫さまを見ただれもが、彼女が高い地位にある人魚だということがわかるでしょう。

「でも、とても痛いわ！」と、小さな人魚姫は言いました。

「そうでしょうとも。でも、私たちには、きちんとした外見のためには、痛みを我慢しなければならない時もあるのです」と、おばあさまは言いました。

ああ、小さな人魚姫は、これらのりっぱなものを身につけていなかったら、どんなにうれしかったことでしょう。彼女は、自分の庭にある赤い花の方がもっと好きでした。でももちろん、その飾りをとることなどできませんでした。「さようなら！」と彼女は言って、水面へすいすいと泳いで上っていきました。

彼女が頭を水面に出した時、太陽はちょうど沈んだばかりでした。雲はピンクや金色に輝いていました。空のまん中には、宵の明星がくっきりと美しく輝いていました。空気は冷たくて気持ちよく、海はガラスのようでした。

The Little Mermaid

A large black ship with three masts lay nearby. Only one sail was up because there was no wind. Many sailors could be seen on the ship, and music and singing could be heard. As the evening grew dark hundreds of pretty lights were lit on board. The little mermaid swam close to the ship. Every time the water raised her up she would look into the ship's window. She saw many well-dressed people. The handsomest was surely a young Prince with large black eyes. He looked to be about sixteen years old at the most. Just like the little mermaid, this was his birthday too. The ship was the scene of his birthday party. On board, the sailors were dancing. When the Prince came out from inside, many rockets were shot into the air. For a moment the night looked like day. The little mermaid became a little afraid and swam under the water. But soon she came up again to look. It seemed as if all the stars from heaven were falling down on her.

■mast 名マスト、帆柱　■nearby 副すぐ近くに　■well-dressed 形身なりの良い　■scene 名現場　■rocket 名打ち上げ花火　■for a moment 一瞬　■as if まるで〜であるかのように

人魚姫

　三本の帆柱がある大きな黒い船が近くにありました。風がまったくなかったので、帆は一つしかはられていませんでした。船の上にはおおぜいの船乗りがいるのが見え、音楽や歌声が聞こえました。外が暗くなってくると、たくさんの美しい灯りが船にともされました。小さな人魚姫は、船の近くまで泳いで行きました。波が彼女を押し上げるたび、船の窓の中をのぞくことができました。船には、よい身なりの人々がたくさんいました。その中でも、もっともハンサムなのは、間違いなく、大きな黒い目をした若い王子さまでした。彼はせいぜい16歳くらいにしか見えませんでした。小さな人魚姫と同じく、この日は彼の誕生日でした。誕生祝いのパーティーが、船上で催されていたのです。船の上で、船乗りたちが踊っていました。王子さまが中から出てくると、たくさんの花火が空に打ち上げられました。一瞬、夜はまるで昼間のように見えました。小さな人魚姫は少し怖くなって、水の下へもぐりましたが、様子を見るために、すぐにまた水面に出てきました。まるですべての星が天から自分に向かって落ちてきているかのように思えました。

The Little Mermaid

She had never seen such fireworks. Large suns turned in fast circles, throwing off fiery colors. And the flat, quiet sea was like a mirror in which you could see everything. It was so bright on the ship that you could see every face clearly. Oh, how handsome the young Prince looked. He was laughing and smiling and shaking hands while the music continued into the night.

It grew late, but the little mermaid could not take her eyes from the ship and the handsome Prince. Now the lights and the fireworks were put out, and things were quieter. But from deep down in the sea there came a low sound. It seemed to grow louder. Still, she rested on the surface, moving up and down with the water and looking into the ship's window. Then the ship began to move faster as the sailors raised the sails. From far away she could see the lightning from a storm.

■firework 名花火　■fiery 形燃えるように赤い　■so ~ that 非常に~なので…　■shake hand 握手をする　■put out (明かり・火を)消す　■rest on ~の上に載っている　■far away 遠く離れて　■lightning 名稲光

人魚姫

　彼女はこのような花火を見たことがありませんでした。太陽のように大きな花火がくるくると回り、火のように赤い火花を飛ばしていました。そして、平らで穏やかな海面は鏡のようで、そこにすべてが映し出されていました。船の上はとても明るかったので、人々の顔がはっきりと見えました。ああ、若い王子さまはなんとハンサムに見えたことでしょう。王子さまは、音楽が夜まで続く中、笑ったり、ほほえんだり、人々と握手をしたりしていました。

　夜も遅くなってきましたが、小さな人魚姫は、その船とハンサムな王子さまから目を離すことができませんでした。今はもう船の灯りと花火は消え、まわりは静かになりました。しかし、海の奥底から、低い音が聞こえてきました。その音は大きくなってくるようでした。それでも彼女は水面に浮かんだまま、波によって上下に動かされながら、船の窓をのぞきこんでいました。それから、船の動きが速くなりました。船乗りたちが帆を上げたからです。遠くの方に、彼女は嵐による稲妻を見ることができました。

The Little Mermaid

And a fearful storm it was. The large ship rolled up and down on the angry ocean. The water rose like great black mountains and looked as if it might cover the ship. But the ship was like a duck and it floated on top of the water. The little mermaid was enjoying the show, but the sailors were not. Then, as wave after wave hit the poor ship, it began to come apart. First one piece of wood then another started to break. The ship turned on its side and the water rushed in. Now the little mermaid saw that they were in danger. She had to watch out for all the pieces of broken ship now in the water. For a moment it was quite dark and she could see nothing. Then in the lightning of the storm she could see everyone falling and rolling into the water. She looked especially for the young Prince and saw him sinking into the deep sea. This made her happy because now he would come to visit her. But then she realized that human beings cannot live under water; he would die before he reached her father's palace.

■fearful 形恐ろしい　■roll 動（船が）横揺れする　■come apart ばらばらになる
■on one's side 横倒しになって　■rush in ドッと押し寄せる　■watch out 気を付ける
■roll into 転がり込む　■sink into ～に沈む

人魚姫

　それは、恐ろしい嵐でした。その大きな船は、怒り狂う海で上下に揺れていました。海水は巨大な黒い山のように盛り上がり、船を覆ってしまいそうに見えました。けれども船はアヒルのように、波の頂点に浮かんでいました。小さな人魚姫はその光景を楽しんで見ていましたが、船乗りたちはそれどころではありませんでした。それから、波が次から次へとあわれな船を襲ったので、船はバラバラになってきました。初めに一片の木材が、次に別の木材がはがれ始めました。船は横倒しになり、海水が流れ込みました。小さな人魚姫には、船に乗っている人々に危険が迫っていることがわかりました。壊れた船からいろいろなものが流れてきていたので、彼女はそれに注意しなければなりませんでした。一瞬あたりは真っ暗になり、何も見えませんでしたが、次の瞬間、嵐の稲妻があたりを照らすと、船に乗っていた人々がみんな海へ転げ落ちていくのが見えました。彼女は王子さまがどこにいるのか探していると、彼が深い海へと沈んでいくのが見えました。小さな人魚姫は、これで王子さまが彼女のもとを訪れることができると思い、うれしくなりました。けれども、人間は水の中では生きられないということを思い出しました。王子さまはお父さまの宮殿に着く前に死んでしまうでしょう。

The Little Mermaid

Oh no! He must not die. So she swam among the pieces of ship looking for him. She seemed to forget the danger that she was in. She ducked below the water and came up again next to him. He had no more power in his arms and legs, and his eyes were closed. Surely he would have died if the little mermaid had not saved him. She held his head above the water, and let the waves take them away.

When morning came the storm had passed. There was nothing left of the ship. The sun rose red from the water. The Prince's face regained some color but his eyes were still closed. The mermaid kissed his handsome forehead and pulled back his hair. He looked just like the statue down in her little garden. She kissed him again and longed that he might live.

■look for 〜を探す　■duck 動 ひょいと水に潜る　■surely 副 間違いなく　■A would have 〜 if B had... もしBが…してなければAは〜だっただろう　■let 動 〜させる　■take away 連れ去る　■regain 動 〜を取り戻す　■forehead 名 額　■pull back 〜を後方へ退ける

人魚姫

　なんということでしょう！　王子さまを死なせるわけにはいきません。小さな人魚姫は王子さまを探して、船の破片の間を泳ぎました。彼女は自分がどんなに危険な状況にいるのか、忘れているかのようでした。彼女は水の下にもぐり、王子さまの横に浮き上がってきました。彼の腕と脚にはもう力が残っておらず、目は閉じたままでした。もし小さな人魚姫が助けていなければ、彼はきっと死んでいたことでしょう。彼女は彼の頭を水の上に持ち上げたまま、波の動きに二人の身をまかせました。

　夜が明けると、嵐はすでに去っていました。船は影も形もなくなっていました。真っ赤な太陽が海から昇ってきました。王子さまの顔には少し生気がもどってきましたが、目はまだ閉じたままでした。人魚姫は王子さまの美しいひたいにキスをし、髪を後ろにまとめてあげました。王子さまは、彼女の小さな庭にある像にそっくりでした。ふたたび彼にキスをし、彼が生きていてくれるように願いました。

The Little Mermaid

And now in front of her she saw land. The high, snowy mountains looking like beautiful clouds. Near the shore were lovely green forests. In front stood a white building. It looked like a church. Lemon and orange trees grew in the garden. At that point there was a small bay; the shore had fine white sand. She swam there with the handsome Prince and laid him on the sand. She made sure that his head was higher than his body in the warm sunshine.

And now the bells in the white building started ringing. A number of girls then came walking through the garden. The little mermaid swam out behind some high rocks in the water so that none could see her. There she watched to see who would come to the poor Prince.

It wasn't long before a young girl walked by. At first, she was afraid when she saw him; but only for a moment. Then she ran to find some other people. The little mermaid could see the Prince come to life again. He smiled at the girl and those around him. But he did not smile at the mermaid, because of course he didn't know that she saved him. When they carried him away into a large building she felt very sad. She swam down under the water and returned to her father's palace.

■point 名突端　■laid 動lay（〜を寝かせる）の過去形　■swim out 泳ぎ出る　■walk by 通り掛かる　■come to life again 意識を取り戻す　■carry 〜 away 〜を運び去る

人魚姫

　その時、小さな人魚姫の目の前に陸地が見えました。高い、雪をいただいた山々は、美しい雲のようでした。岸の近くには美しい緑の森があり、その前には白い建物がありました。それは教会のように見えました。その庭には、レモンやオレンジの木が生えていました。そのあたりは小さな湾になっていて、白く細かい砂の海岸がありました。彼女は美しい王子さまをそこまで泳いで連れていき、砂の上に彼を横たえました。王子さまの頭が体より上にくるようにして、暖かい日差しを受けることができるようにしました。

　その時、白い建物でベルが鳴り始めました。それから、多くの少女たちが庭をぬけて歩いてきました。小さな人魚姫は高い岩の後ろへ泳いでいき、だれにも自分を見られないようにしました。彼女はそこから、かわいそうな王子さまのところへだれかが来てくれるのを見守っていました。

　まもなく、一人の若い少女が通りかかりました。その少女は王子さまを見た時、初めは怖いと思いましたが、それもほんのつかの間のことでした。それから少女は他の人を探しに走っていきました。小さな人魚姫は、王子さまにまた意識がもどってくるのを見ました。彼はその少女と、彼のまわりにいる人々にほほえみかけました。けれども、彼は人魚姫にはほほえんでくれませんでした。当然のことですが、王子さまは、彼女が自分の命を救ってくれたことを知らなかったからです。人々が彼を大きな建物の中に運んで行った時、人魚姫はとても悲しく思いました。彼女は海の下へと泳ぎ、お父さまの宮殿へもどりました。

The Little Mermaid

🎧16 She was always more quiet and thoughtful than her sisters but after this she became even more so. When her sisters asked her what she had seen when she went above for the first time, she told them nothing.

On many mornings and evenings she rose to the spot where she had last seen the Prince. She saw how the fruits on the trees grew large and were then picked; she saw how the snow turned to water on the high mountains, but she did not see the Prince. Every time she returned home sadder and sadder. The only thing she enjoyed doing was sitting in her little garden. There, she would put her arms around the pretty statue that looked like the Prince. But she did not take care of her flowers at all. They began to grow long and wild—over the walkways and through the branches and leaves of the trees. Soon it became quite dark and sad under their shade.

■spot 名場所 ■pick 動摘み取る ■sadder and sadder ますます悲しむ ■walkway 名歩道 ■shade 名陰

人魚姫

　小さな人魚姫は、いつもお姉さまたちより静かで物思いにふけることが多かったのですが、海上の世界を経験したあとは、さらにその傾向が強くなりました。お姉さまたちから、初めて水上に行った時に何を見たのかとたずねられても、彼女は何も話しませんでした。

　朝や晩に、彼女はしばしば、王子さまを最後に見た所へもどってみました。木々の実がどんどん大きくなり、それらが摘まれるのを見ましたし、高い山々の雪が溶けて水になるのも見ましたが、王子さまを見ることはありませんでした。家へ帰るたびに、彼女はもっともっと悲しくなっていくのでした。彼女が楽しんだことは、自分の小さな庭に座っていることだけでした。その庭で、小さな人魚姫は、王子さまによく似た美しい像を抱きかかえるのでした。けれども彼女は花の手入れは何もしませんでした。花は伸び放題になり、歩道の上や、木の枝や葉っぱの間までも茂ってしまいました。やがて、彼女の庭は植物の陰になり、とても暗くて寂しい場所になってしまいました。

The Little Mermaid

At last her sadness became too much for her, so she told her story to one of her sisters. Soon the other sisters and several friends also heard it. One of these friends happened to know who the Prince was and everything about him. She had also seen the party on board the ship. She knew where he came from and where his kingdom was.

"Come, little sister!" said the other Princesses. Arm in arm, they all rose in a long row up to the surface. They went to where they knew the Prince's palace stood. It was built of a light, yellow, shining stone. It had wide, marble steps, one of which reached down to the sea. There were beautiful statues all around the building, and lovely gardens and walls. There were high windows that you could look through to see large paintings on the walls. In the middle of the largest room was a big fountain; the water from the fountain went high in the air towards the glass roof and came down again.

■sadness 图悲しみ ■several 形数人の ■kingdom 图王国 ■arm in arm 腕を組んで ■in a row 1列に並んで ■reach down to ～にまで達する ■fountain 图噴水 ■roof 图天井

人魚姫

　とうとう小さな人魚姫の悲しみはあまりにも深くなり、彼女は水上で起こったことを、お姉さまの一人に話しました。その話はすぐに、他のお姉さまたちと数人のお友達にも伝わりました。そのお友達のうちの一人が、たまたま王子さまがだれなのか、そして彼について何でも知っていました。彼女もあの夜、船上でのパーティーを見たのでした。彼女は王子さまがどこから来たか、そして彼の王国がどこにあるのかも知っていました。
　「妹よ、いらっしゃい！」と、他のお姫さまたちは言いました。みんなで腕を組み、長い列になって水面へ上がりました。彼女たちは王子さまの宮殿があるはずのところまで行きました。宮殿は、薄黄色の輝く石でできていました。幅広の大理石の階段がいくつかあり、その一つは海まで続いていました。建物のまわりは美しい数々の像で取り囲まれ、見事な庭園と塀がありました。高い窓からは、室内の壁にかかっている大きな絵画が見えました。一番大きな部屋のまん中には大きな噴水があり、その水はガラスの天井まで噴き上げられると、また下に落ちてくるのでした。

The Little Mermaid

So now she knew where the Prince lived. On many evenings she rose from the sea and swam near his palace; much nearer than the others dared. In fact, she swam up the little palace waterway to a place under the marble wall. Here she used to sit and watch the young Prince, who thought he was alone in the bright moonshine.

Many an evening she saw him sail in his beautiful boat, with music playing. She would watch from behind the green sea plants. Sometimes the wind would catch and blow her silvery hair. When people saw that they thought it was the wings of a lovely white bird.

Many a night, too, she would listen to the fishermen talk while they worked. They spoke very highly of the young Prince and said only good things about him. She was happier than ever that she had saved his life. And she remembered his head resting on her breast and how she had kissed him. But since he knew nothing of this, he could not even dream about her. More and more she began to love mankind.

■waterway 图水路 ■alone 形孤立した ■silvery 形銀のような ■fisherman 图漁師 ■speak highly of 〜を称賛する ■breast 图胸

人魚姫

　これで王子さまがどこに住んでいるのかわかりました。夜になると人魚姫はしばしば水面へ上り、王子さまの宮殿の近くまで泳いでいきました。他のお姫さまたちなら怖くていけないくらい近くまでです。実際のところ、宮殿の小さい水路を上がって、大理石の壁の下まで行きついていたのでした。そこに座って、人魚姫は若い王子さまを見ていたのです。王子さまは、明るい月明かりの下で、そこにいるのは自分一人だけだと思っていました。

　人魚姫は幾晩も、音楽がかなでられている美しい小舟に王子さまが乗って、海に出ているのを見ました。彼女は緑の海草の陰から王子さまを見ていました。時々、彼女の銀色の髪が風になびいていました。人々はそれを見て、美しい白鳥の羽かと思いました。

　また、人魚姫は幾晩も、漁師たちが働きながら話しているのを聞いていました。彼らは若い王子さまのことをほめそやし、悪いことはまったく言いませんでした。彼女は王子さまの命を救ったことを、今までよりももっとうれしく思ったのでした。そして、彼の頭が自分の胸にもたれかかっていたこと、彼にどのようにキスをしたかを思い出していました。けれども王子さまはそんなことは知るよしもなかったので、彼は人魚姫について考えることなどありませんでした。人魚姫は人間のことをますます好きになってきました。

The Little Mermaid

More and more she wanted to be among people. Their world seemed so much greater than her own. They could fly across the sea in ships; go up to the highest mountains; and their land of trees and fields continued farther than her eye could see.

She wanted to know much more. She asked her sisters, but they were not able to answer her questions. So she asked her grandmother, who knew much about the upper world.

"If men do not get drowned," asked the little mermaid, "can they live forever? Don't they die like we do down here in the sea?"

"Yes," said the old lady, "they also must die. In fact, their lives are shorter than ours. We can live to be three hundred years old. But when we die, we disappear forever, like foam upon the water. We do not have immortal souls; we never enter into a new life. We are like the green sea rushes—if they are cut down, they cannot grow again. But men are different. They have souls which always live— even after the body is lying in the earth.

■upper 形上の　■get drowned 溺死する　■in fact 実際には　■disappear 動存在しなくなる　■foam 名泡　■immortal 形不滅の　■rush 名イグサ

人魚姫

　人魚姫は、もっともっと人間の仲間になりたいと思いました。人間の世界は人魚の世界よりもずっと大きいように感じました。人間は船で海を飛ぶように航海することができ、一番高い山に登ることができ、木や平原に恵まれた人間の土地は、人魚姫が見ることができるよりももっと先まで続いていました。

　人魚姫は人間についてもっと知りたいと思い、お姉さまたちに聞いてみましたが、彼女たちは人魚姫の質問に答えることはできませんでした。そこで、人魚姫はおばあさまにたずねました。おばあさまは水上の世界について、もっとよく知っていたからです。

　「もし人間がおぼれなければ」と、人魚姫は聞きました。「彼らは永遠に生きることができるのでしょうか？　人間は海底にいる私たちのようには死なないのですか？」

　「そんなことはありません」と、おばあさまは言いました。「人間も死にます。それどころか、人間の寿命は私たちより短いのです。人魚は300歳まで生きることができますが、死んだら、水上の泡のように、永遠に消えてしまいます。私たちは永遠の魂をもっていないし、新しい命となることはけっしてできないのですよ。人魚は海の緑の植物のようなもので、もし刈り取られてしまったら、二度と生えてこないのです。けれども人間はちがいます。人間の魂は死ぬことがなく、体が死んでしまっても生き続けるのです。

The Little Mermaid

"They rise up through the clear air to the shining stars. As we rise out of the sea to the land of men, so men's souls rise to beautiful unknown places which we will never know."

"Why do we not have an immortal soul?" asked the little mermaid sadly. "I would gladly give my hundreds of years to be a human being for a single day; then I might hope to live in the world above the sky!"

"You must not trouble yourself about that," said the grandmother. "We have a much better and happier life than mankind above."

"So I shall die and disappear like foam? Hear no more music of the sea? No more pretty flowers and red sun? You mean there is nothing I can do to win an immortal soul?"

"There is!" said the old grandmother. "Only if a man grew to love you more dearly than anything else in the world. If he loved you with all his heart and soul; and if, before a priest, you both promised to be true for now and forever, then his soul would become yours.

■gladly 副喜んで　■human being 人間　■trouble oneself about ～のことを心配する　■dearly 副心から　■priest 名司祭　■promise 動約束する

人魚姫

　人間の魂は透明な空を昇って、輝く星のところまで行くのです。人魚が海を出て人間の土地へ行くように、人間の魂は、私たちが知ることができない、どこか美しい場所へ昇っていくのです」

　「人魚はなぜ不滅の魂をもっていないのですか？」と、小さな人魚姫は悲しそうにたずねました。「もしたった一日でも人間になれるのなら、私は自分の何百年の寿命でも喜んで手放すでしょうに。もしそうできたら、空の上の世界に住みたいわ！」
　「そんなことを考えるのはおよしなさい」と、おばあさまは言いました。「人魚は、地上に住んでいる人間よりもずっと幸せに暮らしているのですからね」
　「それでは、私が死んだら泡のように消えてしまうのですか？　海がかなでる音楽も聞けなくなるのですか？　きれいなお花も、真っ赤な太陽も見ることができないのですか？　不滅の魂を得るために私ができることは何もない、とおっしゃるのですか？」
　「あります！」とおばあさまが言いました。「もし人間の男がおまえを世界中のなによりも愛するようになったら、ですけれどね。もし彼がおまえを心の底から愛したなら、そしてもし司祭さまの前で二人が今も、そして永遠に愛することを約束したなら、彼の魂はおまえのものになるでしょう。

The Little Mermaid

"Only then could you share that happiness that comes to human beings. He would have given you a soul, and yet kept his own. But that can never be! We are different from them. A thing of beauty like your fish's tail is thought to be ugly by people; because they know no better. Up there one must have two strange things called legs to be thought handsome!"

Then the little mermaid looked sadly at her fish's tail.

"We should be happy the way we are," said the old lady, "and really enjoy the three hundred years we have to live. I'm telling you we have a nice long time. Why don't we have a Court dance this very evening!"

Indeed it was a beautiful sight, one that you would never see on earth. The walls of the large dance hall were of clear, thick glass. Hundreds of giant green and red sea shells were hanging on both sides. Bright blue lights made the room shine through the walls and into the sea around. Countless fish of all sizes and colors swam by to look.

■share 動共有する ■yet 副けれども ■ugly 形醜い ■know no better そこまで頭が回らない ■court dance 宮廷舞踊 ■sight 名眺め ■thick 形厚い ■countless 形数え切れないほどの

人魚姫

そうなって初めて、おまえは人間にしか味わえない幸せを彼と分かち合うことができるのです。彼はおまえに魂をくれますが、彼自身の魂はそのまま残ります。けれども、そんなことには決してなりません！ 人魚は人間とはちがうのですから。おまえの美しいしっぽは、人間にはみにくいものとしか考えられません。彼らにはわからないのです。上の世界では、人間は脚と呼ばれる不思議な二本のものが体についていないと、美しいとは思われないのですよ！」

すると小さな人魚姫は、自分のしっぽを悲しそうに見ました。

「私たちはありのままの自分を幸せと思うべきです」とおばあさまは言いました。「そして私たちの300年の寿命を楽しむべきなのです。よくお聞きなさい、私たちにはすばらしく長い時間があるのですよ。今晩は宮殿で舞踏会を開きましょう！」

それは本当に美しい眺めで、地上ではけっして見られないようなものでした。大きなダンスホールの壁は、透明な、厚いガラスでできていました。何百もの巨大な緑や赤の貝殻が両側からぶら下がっていました。部屋の明るい青い灯りが壁を通して輝き、まわりの海も明るくしました。さまざまな大きさと色の魚たちが、数えきれないくらいたくさん見にきました。

The Little Mermaid

Through the great ballroom ran a broad stream; on this the mermen and mermaids danced to their own pretty songs. Such lovely voices are unknown on earth. The little mermaid's voice was the sweetest of all. For a moment her heart was glad. She knew she had the prettiest voice of all living things—on the earth or in the sea. But soon her thoughts turned back to the world above her. She couldn't forget the handsome Prince, nor could she forget that she didn't have, like him, an immortal soul. So she left her father's palace during the party and sat sadly in her garden.

Here she heard the sound of a ship's bell coming down through the water. "I know he is sailing up above—he whom I love more than my mother or father: he to whom my heart wants to belong. I will do everything I can to win him and an immortal soul! While my sisters are dancing in the palace, I will go to the Sea-witch. I have always been afraid of her before, but maybe now she can help me," she thought.

■merman 名男の人魚　■during 前（期間の）間に　■whom 関 〜するところの人
■witch 名魔女

人魚姫

　大きなダンスホールの中に、一筋の幅広い水の流れがありました。そこで、人魚の男女が美しい人魚の歌にあわせて踊りました。こんなに美しい声は地上では考えられないものでした。その中でも、小さな人魚姫の声は一番美しいものでした。しばしの間、人魚姫は歌うことを楽しんでいました。自分がこの世で、地上も海底の世界も含めた中で、一番美しい声をもっていることを知っていたからです。けれどもすぐに、人魚姫は地上の世界のことを考えてしまいました。人魚姫はハンサムな王子さまのこと、そして、自分が王子さまのように不滅の魂をもっていないことを忘れることができなかったのです。彼女は舞踏会の最中にお父さまの宮殿を出て、自分の庭に悲しい気持ちで座っていました。

　そこへ、船の鐘の音が水を通して聞こえてきました。「王子さまが今、海の上を航海しているのだわ。私が、お父さまやお母さまより愛するあの方が。私が心をお寄せしているあの方が。あの方が私を愛するようになるためなら、そして不滅の魂を手に入れるためなら、どんなことでもするわ！　お姉さまたちが宮殿で踊っている間に、私は人魚の魔法使いのところへ行こう。今までは魔法使いのことをいつもおそれていたけれど、彼女なら今、私を助けてくれるかもしれない」と人魚姫は考えました。

The Little Mermaid

So the little mermaid swam out of her part of the sea. She swam towards the dangerous turning water where the Sea-witch lived. She'd never been there before. No flowers or sea plants grew there; only the cold, gray sea bottom. Then she saw the turning water which pulled down everything near it into the deep. On the other side was where the Sea-witch lived. The witch's home was in a very strange forest; a forest of tree snakes—half animal, half plant—called polypi. These terrible things tried to catch and hold anything that came near. She could see the bones of fish, humans, and even another mermaid in these polypi. She had to swim through them and the turning water to reach the Sea-witch's house. She became very afraid and wanted to go home. But then she thought of the Prince, and her strength came back. She tied her hair so that the polypi could not catch it. Then she crossed her arms and swam as fast as she could. She did it!

■turning 名回転、旋回　■sea bottom 海底　■polypi 名polypus（ポリプ）の複数形
■strength 名力、強さ

人魚姫

　そして、小さな人魚姫は、海の中のなじみ深いところから出ていきました。人魚姫は、魔法使いの住んでいる危険な渦に向かって泳ぎました。そこには今まで行ったことがありませんでした。そこでは花も植物も育たず、冷たく、灰色の砂底があるだけでした。それから、人魚姫は、そばにあるものすべてを底にひきずりこんでしまう渦を見ました。魔法使いが住んでいるのは、その先なのです。魔法使いの家はひどく奇妙な森の中にありました。体が半分動物で半分植物の、ポリプと呼ばれる木のヘビの森です。この恐ろしい生き物は、そばに寄ってくるものなら何でもつかまえようとし、つかまえたものは離しませんでした。人魚姫には、これらのポリプにつかみとられてしまった魚や人間の骨、それから他の人魚の骨さえ見えました。魔法使いの家に行くためには、人魚姫はポリプと渦の中を泳いで通りぬけなければならなかったのです。人魚姫はとても怖くなり、家へ帰りたくなりました。けれども、王子さまのことを考えると、力がまたもどってきました。人魚姫は自分の髪を結び、ポリプにつかまれないようにしました。それから腕を組み、できるだけ速く泳ぎました。そして、ついにそこを通りぬけることができたのです！

The Little Mermaid

Now she came to a large, dirty and dark place in the woods. Here were fat, ugly water-snakes floating around. In the middle of this space was a house. It was built from the bones of sailors. Here sat the Sea-witch; a toad was eating from her mouth; the fat water-snakes were moving around her body.

"I know what you want!" said the Sea-witch; "you are a foolish girl! But you shall have your own way, for you will get into trouble, my pretty Princess. You no longer want your fish's tail, eh? You want to walk around on legs like men, do you, so that the young Prince will fall in love with you? You want him and an immortal soul at the same time!"

Then the witch let out a fearfully loud laugh; the toad and the snakes fell to the ground.

■toad 名ヒキガエル ■foolish 形愚かな ■have one's own way 自分の思いどおりにする ■get into trouble 面倒を起こす ■no longer もはや〜でない ■let out（声を）上げる ■fearfully 副恐ろしいほどに

人魚姫

　それから人魚姫は、森の中にある、大きな、薄汚れて暗いところへ来ました。そこには、太ったみにくいミズヘビがただよっていました。そこのまん中に、一軒の家がありました。その家は、船乗りたちの骨でできていました。そこに人魚の魔法使いが座っていました。ヒキガエルが魔法使いの口からエサをもらっており、太ったミズヘビたちが彼女の体のまわりにうごめいていました。

　「おまえが何を欲しいかは、わかっているよ！」と魔法使いは言いました。「バカな子だね！　でも、あんたが好きなようにするがいいさ。困ったことにはなるがね、きれいなお姫さま。もう魚のしっぽはいらないんだってねえ？　人間のような脚で歩きまわって、あの若い王子がおまえを愛するようになってほしいんだろう？　おまえは、あの王子と不滅の魂をいっしょに手に入れたいんだね！」

　それから魔法使いは恐ろしい声で大きく笑ったので、ヒキガエルとミズヘビたちは地面に落ちてしまいました。

The Little Mermaid

"You have come at the right time," said the witch; "If you had come tomorrow, I couldn't have helped you for another year. I will make you a magic drink. Then you must swim to land, sit on the shore and drink all of it before sunrise. Then your tail will become two nice legs. But it will hurt; it will feel like a sword is cutting you in half. Those who see you will say you are the loveliest girl alive. You will be able to walk and dance beautifully; but every step will feel painful. If you want to suffer all this, I have the power to help you."

"I do," said the little mermaid, her voice shaking; she thought of the Prince and of having an immortal soul.

"But remember," said the witch, "once you have a human form you can never become a mermaid again! You will never be able to dive down through the water to your father's palace. And if you fail to win the Prince's love—his love for you above all things—then you will not gain an immortal soul. The morning after he marries another, your heart will break: And your body will become like foam upon the water."

■sunrise 图日の出　■sword 图剣　■alive 形生きている者のうちで　■painful 形痛みを伴う　■fail 動失敗する　■gain 動〜を得る

人魚姫

「おまえさんはちょうどいい時に来たよ」と魔法使いは言いました。「もし明日来ていたら、来年までおまえを助けてやることはできなかっただろう。おまえに魔法の飲み物をつくってやろう。それからおまえは陸まで泳いで行き、岸に座って、日が昇る前にそれを飲み干さなければならない。そうしたらおまえのしっぽは二本のりっぱな脚になるのさ。けれど、それはひどく痛むぞ。まるで剣がおまえの体をまっぷたつに切りさくような痛さじゃ。おまえさんを見る人は、おまえはこの世で一番美しい娘だと言うだろう。おまえは歩けるようになり、見事に踊れるようになるだろう。だが、一歩踏むごとに足がひどく痛むだろう。それでもいいと言うのなら、私にはおまえさんを助けてやる力があるのじゃ」

「やります」と小さな人魚姫は言いましたが、その声は震えていました。人魚姫は、王子さまのこと、そして不滅の魂をもつことを考えました。

「忘れちゃいけないのは」と魔法使いは言いました。「いったん人間の体になったら、人魚には二度ともどれないことだ！ おまえは水の中を下まで泳いで、おまえの父親の宮殿まで行くことは、もうできなくなるんだ。それから、もし王子の愛、ほかのなによりもおまえを愛するくらいの愛を手に入れられなければ、不滅の魂を手に入れることはできないぞ。王子が他の娘と結婚した翌朝、おまえの心ははりさけ、体は水に浮かぶ泡のようなものになってしまうんだ」

The Little Mermaid

"So be it!" said the little mermaid, but she was so afraid.

"You must pay me too," said the witch, "and it will not be a small thing that I demand. You have the loveliest voice of all things here at the bottom of the sea. You believe you can win the Prince with that voice, I know. But no, you must give that voice to me. I want to have the finest part of you in return for my magic drink. For in my magic drink I must include my own blood."

"But if you take my voice," asked the little mermaid, "what will I have left?"

"Your lovely body," said the witch, "your light walk and your speaking eyes. I think you can fool a man's heart with those. Well! Do you have the nerve? Put out your little tongue and I will cut it off as payment; and you shall have the magic drink!"

■So be it. それならそれで仕方ない。　■demand 動 要求する　■in return for ～に対する見返りとして　■include 動 ～を含める　■nerve 名 度胸　■put out 外に出す　■payment 名 報酬

人魚姫

「それでもかまいません!」と人魚姫は言いましたが、彼女はとても怖かったのです。

「それと、私にも支払いをしてもらうよ」と魔法使いは言いました。「私が欲しいのはちっぽけなものじゃない。おまえはこの海の底で一番美しい声をしている。おまえはその美しい声で王子の心をつかめると信じていることくらい、こっちはお見通しさ。だが、だめだね、おまえはその声を私によこさなければいけないのじゃ。魔法の飲み物へのお返しに、おまえの体の一番よいところが欲しい。魔法の飲み物の中に、自分の血を入れなければならないんだからね」

「でも、もしあなたが私の声をとりあげてしまったら」と小さな人魚姫はたずねました。「私には何が残るのでしょうか?」

「おまえの美しい体さ」と魔法使いは言いました。「おまえの軽やかな歩きと、いろんなことを伝えられる目さ。そいつを使えば、男の心をだますことができるはずじゃ。さて! おまえさんにはその勇気があるかな? その小さい舌をお出し。それを代金として切り取ってやるから。そうしたらおまえは魔法の飲み物を手に入れることができるのじゃ!」

The Little Mermaid

[27] "All right, then!" said the little mermaid. The witch started a fire to make her magic drink. "A clean pot is best," she said. Then she picked up two or three snakes and used them to clean the pot. After that, she cut open her own breast and her black blood dropped into the pot. Every moment she added something fresh into the pot. Soon it was quite hot; the sounds were loud and the smells were strong. At last, when the drink was ready, it looked like the clearest water!

"Here you are!" said the witch. Then she cut out the tongue of the little mermaid. Now the mermaid could not speak at all; nor could she sing.

"If the polypi touch you on your way out," said the witch, "just throw one drop of this magic drink on them. It will kill them!" But the little mermaid didn't need to do this. When the polypi saw the magic drink in her hand, they backed away in fear. Very soon she passed through the forest and the dangerous turning water.

■start a fire 火をおこす　■pick up 手に取る　■add 動加える　■ready 形用意ができて　■on one's way out 出ていく途中で　■back away 後ずさりする

人魚姫

「わかりました!」と小さな人魚姫は言いました。魔法使いは、魔法の飲み物をつくるために火をおこしました。「清潔な鍋が一番だからね」と言って、彼女は二、三匹のミズヘビをつかむと、それで鍋をきれいにしました。そのあと、魔法使いが自分の胸を切ると、黒い血が鍋の中にしたたり落ちました。彼女は次から次へと、何か新鮮なものを鍋に加えました。すぐに鍋はとても熱くなり、その音は大きく、臭いはとても強くなりました。ついにその飲み物ができた時、それはまったく透明な水のように見えました!

「ほら、これだよ!」と魔法使いは言いました。それから魔法使いは、小さな人魚姫の舌を切り取りました。今や人魚姫は話すことがまったくできなくなってしまいました。歌も歌えなくなりました。

「おまえが出ていく時に、ポリプがもしおまえに触ろうとしたら」と魔法使いは言いました。「あいつらにこの魔法の飲み物を一滴投げつけるんだ。そうしたらあいつらは死んじまうからね!」けれど、小さな人魚姫はそうする必要はありませんでした。ポリプが人魚姫の手の中にある魔法の飲み物を見ると、彼らは怖がってひっこみました。人魚姫はとても短い時間で森と危険な渦を通りぬけました。

The Little Mermaid

She could see her father's palace. The lights in the long dance hall were off; everyone inside was sleeping. But she dared not visit them, now that she couldn't speak. Now she was going to leave them forever. Her heart felt as if it might break in two. She entered the garden and picked a flower from each of her sister's flower beds. Then she threw a thousand kisses towards the palace and rose through the dark waters.

She arrived at the Prince's palace shortly before the sun rose. She went to the marble steps and sat down. Then she drank the magic drink. It felt as though a two-sided sword was cutting through her body. She was in great pain and lay there like a dead person.

When the sun came over the sea she woke up. The pain was very sharp but in front of her stood the handsome young Prince. He looked at her with his dark eyes for a long time; finally, she looked down and noticed that her fish tail had become pretty white legs. But she was wearing no clothes and covered herself with her long, thick hair.

■off 副（スイッチが）切れて　■shortly before ちょっと前に　■as though まるで〜であるかのように　■two-sided 形両側がある　■dark eyes 黒い瞳　■notice 動気が付く

人魚姫

　人魚姫はお父さまの宮殿を見ることができました。長いダンスホールの灯りはぜんぶ消えており、中にいる人々は眠っていました。しかし、彼女はあえて彼らのところに行こうとはしませんでした。もう話すことができなかったのですから。今から人魚姫は永遠に家族を残して去って行くのです。彼女の心は、まるで二つにはりさけそうに感じました。人魚姫は庭へ行き、お姉さまたちの花壇からそれぞれ一輪ずつ花を摘みました。それから宮殿に向かってたくさんのキスを送り、暗い水の中を水面へと上がって行きました。

　人魚姫は日が昇る寸前に王子さまの宮殿へ着きました。彼女は大理石の階段へ行き、そこに座りました。それから魔法の飲み物を飲みました。それはまるで両刃の剣が体を切りさいていくかのように感じられました。人魚姫は激しい痛みを感じ、死んだ人のようにそこに横たわっていました。

　太陽が海の上を照らした時、人魚姫は目を覚ましました。痛みは激しかったのですが、目の前には、あのハンサムな若い王子さまが立っていました。王子さまはその黒い瞳で、人魚姫のことを長いあいだ見つめていました。とうとう彼女が下を見ると、自分のしっぽが、美しく白い脚になっているのに気がつきました。けれども人魚姫は何も着ていなかったので、長く、豊かな髪で自分の体を隠しました。

The Little Mermaid

The Prince asked who she was and how she got there. But she could only look at him with her dark blue eyes, for she couldn't speak. Then he took her by the hand and led her into the palace. As the witch said, every step was like walking on sword points. But she accepted the pain. Hand in hand they walked along, while others watched them. They were surprised at her beauty and light, floating movements.

Now she was dressed in the most costly silk clothes. None in the palace was as lovely as her. But she could neither sing nor speak. Other young ladies, dressed in gold and silk, came and sang to the Prince and his parents. One of them sang more sweetly than the others. The Prince seemed quite happy. This troubled the little mermaid, for she knew that her voice was far prettier, and she thought: "Oh, that he might know the truth—that I have given away my voice forever to be near him!"

■get there そこに到着する　■sword point 剣の先　■accept 動受け入れる　■hand in hand 手をとり合って　■walk along（前方へ）歩く　■costly 形高価な

人魚姫

　王子さまは彼女がだれなのか、そしてどうやってここまで来たのかたずねました。しかし人魚姫は、深く青い目で彼を見ることしかできませんでした。話すことができなかったからです。それから王子さまは彼女の手をとり、宮殿の中へ連れていきました。人魚の魔法使いが言った通り、一歩ごとに、まるで剣先の上を歩いているかのようでした。でも、人魚姫はその痛みを受け入れました。二人が手に手をとって歩いている間、他の人々は二人を見ていました。みんな人魚姫の美しさと、軽く、まるで浮かんでいるような動き方に驚きました。

　人魚姫はとても高価な絹の服を着せてもらいました。宮殿の中で、彼女ほど美しい人はいませんでした。けれども、人魚姫は歌うことも話すこともできませんでした。他の若い婦人たちは、金や絹のドレスを着てやって来て、王子さまとそのご両親のために歌いました。その中の一人は、特にすばらしく歌いました。王子さまはとても幸せそうでした。それは、人魚姫の心を苦しめました。自分の声はもっときれいだということを知っていたからです。そして彼女は考えました。「ああ、王子さまが真実を知っていたら。私が彼のそばにいるために、自分の声を永遠に失くしてしまったことを知っていたら！」

The Little Mermaid

Then the other girls danced some light and pretty dances to lovely music. At this the little mermaid stood up. She lifted her lovely white arms and began to float across the floor as none other had done before. Every moment made her beauty more clear. Her eyes also spoke more deeply to the heart than the songs of the other girls.

Everyone came to like her, especially the Prince. She danced more and more; though each step she took was very painful. The Prince declared that she should always be with him. She was allowed to sit outside his door.

Presently, he had her dressed in men's clothing so that she might ride horses with him. They rode together through the pretty-smelling woods; where green branches touched their shoulders and little birds sang among the fresh green leaves. She also walked right up the high mountains with him. Although blood came from her feet, she only tried to laugh at her suffering. She followed him higher until they could see the clouds floating like birds below them.

■none other 他のだれも〜ない　■declare 動 宣言する　■presently 副 やがて　■so that 〜できるように　■rode 動 ride（乗馬する）の過去形

人魚姫

　それから、ほかの娘たちが、美しい曲に合わせて軽やかにかわいらしく踊りました。この時、小さな人魚姫は立ち上がりました。彼女は美しい白い腕を上げ、他の人たちが今までにやったことがない様子で、床の上からまるで浮き上がっているかのように踊りました。その一瞬一瞬が、人魚姫の美しさをさらに際立たせました。彼女の目は、他の娘たちの歌よりもっと強く心に訴えかけました。

　みんなが、特に王子さまは、人魚姫のことを好きになりました。人魚姫はもっともっと踊りました。けれども、ステップを踏むたびにひどく足が痛みました。王子さまは、彼女はいつも自分といっしょにいるべきだと宣言しました。人魚姫は王子さまの部屋のドアの外に座ることを許されました。

　やがて王子さまは人魚姫に男の服を着せ、自分といっしょに馬に乗ることができるようにしました。二人はいっしょに、よい香りのする森を馬に乗って駆け抜けました。森では、緑の枝が二人の肩に触れ、小鳥がさわやかな緑の葉っぱの間で歌っていました。人魚姫は王子さまといっしょに、高い山にも登りました。人魚姫の足には血がにじんでいましたが、彼女はその痛みを笑ってやり過ごそうとしました。人魚姫は王子さまの後について、二人の下に雲が鳥のように浮かんでいるのが見えるような高い所まで登ったのでした。

The Little Mermaid

At night, while others slept in the Prince's palace, she would walk out on the broad marble steps. For it cooled her burning feet to stand in the cold sea water. She thought of her family and friends far below in the water.

One night her sisters rose up arm in arm. They sang so sadly as they swam in the water. They saw each other. Her sisters then told her how sad she had made them by leaving.

After that, they visited her every night. Once, a long way off, she saw her aged grandmother; she had not come to the surface for many years. She also saw her father, the Sea-King. They held out their hands to her but dared not come so close to land as her sisters.

Every day she became dearer to the Prince. He loved her as one might love a dear, good child; but he never thought about making her his wife. Yet his wife she must become; if not she would disappear like the foam on the morning after he married another.

"Do you love me most of all?" the eyes of the mermaid seemed to ask him when he kissed her forehead.

■walk out 歩いて外へ出る　■a long way off ずっと先である　■become dear to（人）にとっていとしい存在になる　■another 代もう一人　■most of all 何よりも

人魚姫

　夜になり、王子さまの宮殿の人々が寝ている間、人魚姫は広い大理石の階段まで歩いていくのでした。冷たい海水の中で、燃えるように痛む足を冷やすことができたからです。人魚姫は水の下にいる自分の家族や友達のことを考えました。

　ある夜、人魚姫のお姉さまたちが、腕と腕を組んで上がってきました。お姉さまたちは泳ぎながら、とても悲しそうに歌いました。人魚姫とお姉さまたちは顔を見合わせました。お姉さまたちは、人魚姫が去ってしまったあと、とても悲しい思いをしていることを伝えました。

　それからは、お姉さまたちは毎晩、人魚姫のもとを訪れました。ある時、人魚姫はとても遠くの方に、年老いたおばあさまを見かけました。おばあさまはとても長い間、水上に来たことがありませんでした。人魚姫には、お父さまである人魚の王も見えました。二人は手を人魚姫の方へ差し伸べていましたが、お姉さまたちのように陸の近くまで来ようとはしませんでした。

　日がたつにつれて、人魚姫は王子さまにとってさらに大切な人となっていきました。王子さまは彼女のことを、大切な、かわいい子どもをかわいがるように愛していました。けれども王子さまは、人魚姫を自分の妻にすることは考えたことがありませんでした。それでも、人魚姫は王子さまの妻になる必要があるのです。そうしないと、王子さまが他の娘と結婚した翌朝、人魚姫は泡のように消えてしまうのです。

　「私のことが何よりも一番お好きですか？」王子さまが人魚姫のひたいにキスをした時、人魚姫の目はそう聞いているように見えました。

The Little Mermaid

"Yes, you are dearest of all to me," said the Prince, "for you have the best heart. You are the kindest to me. You are like a lovely young lady I once saw but shall never see again. I was on a ship that sunk in a storm. The waves brought me ashore near a holy temple, where many young girls were studying. The youngest, who found me on the shore and saved my life, I only saw twice. She is the only one I could love in this world; but you are like her. You almost make me forget her. She belongs to the holy temple; therefore, my good fortune has sent you to me instead, and we will never part."

"Alas! He does not know that it was I who saved his life," thought the little mermaid. "I carried him across the sea to the wood where the holy temple stands. I sat behind the rocks and watched to see if anyone would come. I saw the pretty girl that he loves more than he does me!" The mermaid wanted to cry but she could not. "He says the girl belongs to that holy temple, and will never come out into the world; and they will never meet again. I am with him; I see him every day. I will love him and give my life to him!"

■ashore 副岸へ　■holy temple 聖堂　■fortune 名(幸)運　■alas 間悲しいかな
■see if 〜かどうかを確かめる　■come out 外へ出る

人魚姫

　「ああ、おまえは私にとって一番大切な人だよ」と王子さまは言いました。「おまえはとてもよい心持ちの人だから。私に一番やさしくしてくれる。おまえは私が前に一度会ったきり、もう二度と会えない美しい若い娘によく似ているよ。私が乗っていた船が嵐で沈没したことがあるのだ。波が私を聖堂の近くにある岸まで打ち上げた。その聖堂では、多くの若い娘たちが学んでいた。一番若い娘が私を岸で見つけ、私の命を救ってくれたのだが、彼女のことは二度しか見たことがない。彼女はこの世でただ一人、私が愛することができる人だ。でもおまえは彼女に似ている。おまえは彼女のことをほとんど忘れさせてくれる。彼女は聖堂に属する人だ。だから、きっと私の幸運が、かわりにおまえを私のもとに連れてきてくれたのだろう。私たちはぜったいに離ればなれにはならないよ」

　「ああ！　王子さまは、自分の命を救ったのは私だということを知らないのだ」と小さな人魚姫は思いました。「私が海を横切り、王子さまを聖堂がある森へ運んだ。私は岩の陰に座り、だれか来てくれるかどうか見守っていた。私は、王子さまが私より愛している、あの美しい娘を見たわ！」人魚姫は泣きたかったのですが、そうできませんでした。「王子さまは、あの娘は聖堂に属する人なので、そこからは決して出てこないだろうと言っている。だから二人は二度と会うことはない。王子さまと今いっしょにいるのは私。毎日会っているわ。私は彼を愛し、私の命を彼に捧げるわ！」

The Little Mermaid

But now there was talk that the Prince was to marry. They said he was to take the lovely daughter of the neighboring king to be his wife. That's why he was now preparing to sail away on a fine ship. "The Prince is traveling to see the land of the neighboring king," they said; but everyone knew he was really going to see the king's daughter.

The little mermaid shook her head and smiled. She knew the Prince's thoughts better than the others. "I must travel," he said to her. "I must see this beautiful Princess because my parents want me to; but they shall not force me to marry her. I cannot love her; she is not like the lovely girl in the temple whom you are like. Should I ever choose a bride, I would rather have you, my speechless lovely!" And he kissed her mouth, played with her long hair, and laid his head close to her heart. She dreamed of human happiness and an immortal soul.

■talk 名うわさ　■neighboring 形近隣の　■prepare 動準備する　■shook 動shake（〜を振る）の過去形　■force 動強制する

人魚姫

　ところが、王子さまが結婚するといううわさがささやかれ始めました。王子さまはとなりの国王の美しい娘を妻にめとるというのでした。だから王子さまは今、豪華な船で出航準備をしているのだ、という話でした。「王子さまはとなりの国王の国を見に行くのだ」と人々は言いました。けれども、本当は王さまの娘に会いにいくのだということをだれもが知っていました。

　小さな人魚姫は頭をふり、ほほえみました。彼女は王子さまが考えていることを、ほかのだれよりもよく知っていたからでした。「私は旅に出なければならない」と王子さまは人魚姫に言いました。「私はその美しい姫に会わなければならない。それが私の両親が望むことだから。だが、父上も母上も、私がその姫と結婚することを強いることはできない。私はその姫を愛すことはできない。彼女は、おまえに似た、聖堂にいるあの美しい娘に似ているわけがないからだ。私が花嫁を選ぶとしたら、おまえを選ぶだろう、私のかわいい声が出ない娘よ！」そして王子さまは人魚姫の口にキスをし、その長い髪にやさしく触り、彼女の胸の近くに頭をもたせかけたのでした。人魚姫は、人間の幸福と不滅の魂を夢見ました。

The Little Mermaid

"Surely you are not afraid of the sea, my speechless child!" said he. They were standing together on the fine ship carrying him to the land of the neighboring king. And he talked to her of the sea, of nice days and stormy ones, of the strange fish in the deep and what is down there. She smiled, for she knew better than any human about the bottom of the sea.

In the moonlight, when all on board were asleep, she sat at the side of the ship and looked down through the clear water. She seemed to see her father's palace. High above it stood the old grandmother with her silver crown on her head; she was looking up at the ship's bottom. Then her sisters came up to the surface. They looked at her sadly and moved towards her. She smiled, and would have told them she was well and happy, but a sailor came by just then. Her sisters dived below the waves, and she was no longer sure that she had really seen them.

The next morning the ship sailed into the neighboring king's city. The church bells were ringing; flags flew from the tops of buildings, and the king's soldiers stood holding their shining swords.

■crown 名王冠　■flag 名旗　■flew 動fly (〈旗などが〉はためく) の過去形　■soldier 名兵士

人魚姫

「おまえは本当に海を怖がらないのだね、私の声が出ない子どもよ！」と王子さまは言いました。二人は、隣国の王の国へと王子さまを運ぶ、豪華な船の上にいっしょに立っていました。そして王子さまは人魚姫に、海について、穏やかな日と嵐の日のことや、深い海にいる不思議な魚のこと、海の中に何がいるかなどについて話してくれました。人魚姫はほほえみました。海底については、どんな人間よりも自分の方が一番よく知っていたからです。

月明かりのもと、船に乗っている人々がみんな寝静まっている時、人魚姫は船のへりに座って、澄んだ水を通して下を見ました。お父さまの宮殿が見えるように思いました。宮殿の上には、おばあさまが銀の冠をかぶって立っていました。おばあさまは船の底を見上げていました。それからお姉さまたちが水上に上がって来ました。お姉さまたちは悲しそうに彼女を見て、近づいてきました。人魚姫はほほえみ、自分は元気で幸せにしていると言おうとしたのですが、その時、船乗りが近くに来てしまいました。お姉さまたちは波の下へもぐってしまい、人魚姫はお姉さまたちを本当に見たのかどうか、確信がもてなくなってしまいました。

翌朝、船は隣国の王の住む町へ着きました。教会のベルが鳴り響き、建物の上からは多くの旗がなびき、王さまの兵隊が輝く剣を抱えて立っていました。

The Little Mermaid

Every day brought a large dinner with music and dancing. But the Princess was not yet there. She was being brought up in a holy temple far away, they said. There she was learning things that a good Princess should know. At last she arrived.

Like others, the little mermaid really wanted to see her loveliness. And it was true; a more beautiful face she had never seen. Her skin, her hair, and her dark blue eyes were like those of a goddess.

"It is you!" cried the Prince, "you who saved me when I lay on the sea-shore!" And he held his bride-to-be. "Oh! I am so happy, I don't know what to do!" he said to the mermaid. "My greatest wish has come true. You too will share my happiness, for you love me more than all of them!" And the little mermaid kissed his hand, but already she felt her heart would break. Yes, the morning after his wedding would mean her death.

■loveliness 名愛らしさ　■goddess 名女神　■sea-shore 名海岸　■bride-to-be 名花嫁になる人　■come true （夢などが）実現する　■already 副すでに

人魚姫

　毎日、音楽やダンスをともなう盛大な祝宴が催されました。けれども、王さまの娘のお姫さまは、まだそこにいませんでした。お姫さまは遠く離れた聖堂で育てられているのだ、と人々は言いました。その聖堂で、彼女はすばらしいお姫さまになるために学んでいたのです。そしてとうとう、お姫さまが到着しました。

　他の人々と同じように、小さな人魚姫も、そのお姫さまの美しさをとても見たかったのでした。そして、そのお姫さまが美しいというのは本当でした。その顔は、人魚姫が今までに見たこともないほどの美しさでした。お姫さまの肌、髪の毛、そして深く青い瞳は、まるで女神のようでした。

　「あなたなのですね！」と王子さまが叫びました。「あなたが海岸で横たわっていた私を救ってくれたのですね！」そして王子さまは花嫁となるお姫さまを抱きしめました。「ああ！　私は本当に幸せで、どうしたらいいのかわからない！」と王子さまは人魚姫に言いました。「私の一番大きな願いがかなったのだ。おまえも私の幸せを祝ってくれるね。おまえはだれよりも私のことを愛してくれているのだから！」それから小さな人魚姫は王子さまの手にキスをしましたが、彼女の胸はすでにはりさけそうでした。そうです、王子さまの婚礼の翌朝は、人魚姫の死を意味するのです。

The Little Mermaid

All the bells were ringing and word of their wedding was passing through the city. All the preparations were made in the church. The bride and bridegroom stood before the priest and received his holy words. The little mermaid was dressed in cloth of gold. She stood behind the bride and held her dress. But her ears did not hear the wedding music, nor did her eyes really see the wedding. She thought of her night of death, of all that she lost in this world.

The same evening, the bride and bridegroom went aboard the ship. Guns were fired, flags were waved, and a special bridal room and bed were prepared.

The sails opened up in the light wind, and the ship floated lightly over the ocean. When it became dark, colored lights were lit. The sailors danced happily on board. The little mermaid thought of the first time she had risen above the sea. Then she had seen the same partying. And she danced for them; round and round she turned, floating along the deck like a bird. Never had she danced so beautifully.

■word 名知らせ ■preparation 名準備 ■cloth 名布地 ■bridegroom 名花婿 ■go aboard（船などに）乗る ■bridal 形婚礼の

人魚姫

　すべての鐘が鳴り響き、町中に二人の婚礼のことが知れ渡っていきました。教会ではすべての準備が整いました。花嫁と花婿は司祭さまの前に立ち、神聖なお言葉をいただきました。小さな人魚姫は金の布地でつくられたドレスを着ていました。人魚姫は花嫁の後ろに立ち、お姫さまのドレスのすそを持ち上げていました。けれども、人魚姫の耳には婚礼の音楽は聞こえず、目にも結婚式は本当には見えてはいませんでした。自分が死ぬ夜のこと、そしてこの世で失ったすべてのことを考えていました。

　その日の夕方のこと、花嫁と花婿は船に乗りました。大砲が鳴り響き、旗がはためき、特別な婚礼の部屋とベッドが用意されました。

　船の帆はそよ風に広げられ、船は海の上に軽やかに浮かんでいました。外が暗くなってくると、色とりどりの灯りがともされました。船乗りたちは楽しそうに踊りました。小さな人魚姫は自分が初めて水上に上がって来た時のことを考えていました。その時も同じようなパーティーを見ていました。それから人魚姫は二人のために踊りました。くるくると回転し、小鳥のようにデッキの上を浮かぶように踊りました。人魚姫がそれほど美しく踊ったことはありませんでした。

The Little Mermaid

As always, there was the pain of sharp sword points in her feet, but she didn't think about it. Instead, the pain in her heart was far worse. She knew that this was the last time she would see him; the Prince for whom she had given up her voice, her family and home, and suffered such pain every day. And still he could know nothing of it. This would be the last time she would look at the sea and the stars. Forever after this she would see nothing, for she had no soul and could not get one.

All was joyful on board the ship until after midnight. She danced and laughed with the others but thought of death in her heart. The Prince kissed his lovely bride, and she played with his black hair. Arm in arm they went to rest in their beautiful room.

Later, all was still and dark on board. The little mermaid rested on the side of the ship looking east to where the sun would rise. The first light, she knew, must kill her. Then she saw her sisters rise from the sea. They looked as white as she. Their long fair hair no longer blew in the wind; it had all been cut off.

■far worse はるかに悪い　■give up ～を引き渡す　■joyful 形うれしい　■rest 動休む

人魚姫

　いつものように、鋭い剣先が刺さるような痛みを足に感じましたが、人魚姫はその痛みのことは考えませんでした。それよりも、心の痛みはもっとひどいものでした。人魚姫はこれが王子さまを見る最後の時となることを知っていました。王子さまのために、人魚姫は自分の声も家族も家も捨て、毎日このような痛みに耐えてきました。それなのに、王子さまはそのことを何も知らないのでした。これが人魚姫が海と星を見る最後になるでしょう。これから先、人魚姫は永遠に何も見ることはないでしょう。人魚には魂がなく、それを手に入れることもできないのですから。

　真夜中過ぎまで、船の上の人々はみんな楽しそうにしていました。彼女は他の人々といっしょに踊ったり笑ったりしていましたが、心の中では死のことを考えていました。王子さまは美しい花嫁にキスをし、花嫁は王子さまの黒い髪をなでていました。二人は腕を組んで、自分たちの美しい部屋へ休みに行きました。

　その後、船の上は静まり暗くなりました。小さな人魚姫は船べりで休み、日が昇ってくる東の方を見ていました。最初の光で自分が死ぬことを、人魚姫はわかっていました。その時、彼女はお姉さまたちが海から上がってくるのを見ました。お姉さまたちは彼女と同じくらい白い顔をしていました。お姉さまたちの長く美しい髪は、もはや風になびいてはいませんでした。それはみな切り取られていたのでした。

The Little Mermaid

"We have given it to the Sea-witch so that you may not die tonight! She has given us this small sword! Before the sun rises you must push this sword into the Prince's heart; Then, when his warm blood touches your feet, they will again become a fish's tail and you will once more be a mermaid. Then you may come back to us and live your three hundred years before you die. Please hurry! Either he or you must die before sunrise. Our old grandmother has become so sad that her hair has fallen out; ours has been cut off by the witch. Kill the Prince and come back to us! Hurry! Don't you see the red lines in the sky far away? A few more minutes and the rising sun will kill you." And they sank again beneath the waves.

The little mermaid quietly opened the door to the Prince's room. She saw the beautiful bride asleep with her head on the Prince's breast. She walked to the bed, stood over the Prince, and kissed him while he slept. Then she looked up at the sky which was becoming redder and redder. She then looked at the sword in her hand, and again at the Prince. The Prince, in his dreams, called his bride by name; she alone was in his thoughts. The mermaid's hand was shaking. Should she strike?

■once more もう一度　■beneath 前 ～の真下に　■stand over（人）のそばに立って見下ろす　■call someone by name（人）を名前で呼ぶ　■strike 動 突き刺す

人魚姫

「私たちは髪を人魚の魔法使いにあげました。おまえが今晩死なないように！ 魔法使いは私たちにこの小さな剣をくれたわ！ 日が昇る前に、おまえはこの剣で王子の心臓を刺さないといけません。そして、彼の温かい血がおまえの足に触れた時、それはふたたび魚のしっぽになって、おまえは人魚にもう一度もどることができるのよ。そうしたら、おまえは私たちのところにもどってきて、死ぬまでに300年生きることができるのです。お願いだから、急いで！ 王子かおまえのどちらかが、日が昇る前に死ななければならない。おばあさまはあんまり悲しんだので、髪がぬけてしまったの。私たちの髪は魔法使いに切られたわ。王子を殺して、私たちのところへもどっておいで！ 急いで！ 遠くの空の赤い線がおまえには見えないの？ あと数分で昇ってくる太陽がおまえを殺してしまうのよ」そしてお姉さまたちは波の下へふたたび沈んでいきました。

　人魚姫は、王子さまの部屋へのドアを静かに開けました。美しい花嫁が、彼女の頭を王子さまの胸にもたせかけて眠っているのが見えました。人魚姫はベッドへ歩いていき、王子さまのそばに立ち、寝ている彼にキスをしました。そして、人魚姫はますます赤くなってきている空を見上げました。人魚姫はそれから自分が手にしている剣を見、そしてまた王子さまを見ました。王子さまは夢の中で、花嫁の名前を呼びました。彼の頭の中には花嫁のことしかないのでした。人魚姫の手は震えていました。王子さまを刺すべきでしょうか？

The Little Mermaid

Another moment passed and she threw the sword far away into the waves. They became red where it fell, as if the sea was bleeding. Once again she looked with painful eyes at the Prince. Then she jumped from the ship into the sea, and felt her body changing into foam.

And now the sun rose out of the sea. Its heat fell with gentle warmth upon the cold sea foam, and the little mermaid did not feel the touch of death. She saw the bright sun. Above her were hundreds of beautiful forms with no bodies. They were floating in the air. She could still see the white sails of the ship and the red clouds in the sky.

The voices of the forms were musical; but so heavenly that no human ear could hear them. Nor could any human eye see them. They had no wings but floated in the air because they were so light.

The little mermaid now had a body like theirs. It rose higher and higher from out of the foam.

"To whom have I come?" she cried. Her voice sounded like that of the other beings. It was so heavenly that no earthly music could equal it.

■bleed 動出血する　■fall upon ～の上にかかる　■touch of 様子、気配　■heavenly 形素晴らしい、美しい　■being 名存在[実在]するもの　■earthly 形この世の　■equal 動釣り合う

人魚姫

　次の瞬間、人魚姫は、剣をはるかかなたの波の中に投げました。剣が落ちたあたりの波は赤くなり、まるで海から血が流れているかのようでした。もう一度、人魚姫は、痛む目で王子さまを見ました。それから人魚姫は船から海へ飛び込み、自分の体が泡になっていくのを感じました。

　そして、太陽が海から昇ってきました。その熱はやさしい暖かさで冷たい海の泡の上に伝わり、小さな人魚姫は死の気配を感じませんでした。人魚姫はまぶしい太陽を見ました。上には、何百もの体のない美しいものがありました。それは空中に浮かんでいました。人魚姫は、船の白い帆や空の赤い雲を、まだ見ることができました。

　空に浮かんでいるものたちの声は音楽のようでした。けれども、あまりにもすばらしいので、人間の耳には聞こえず、また、人間には見ることもできないのでした。それには羽がないのに、とても軽いので、空中に浮かんでいたのです。
　小さな人魚姫の体は、今ではそれらと同じようなものになっていました。彼女の体は泡から抜け出て、高く、さらに高く上がっていきました。
　「どなたのところへ私は来たのでしょうか？」と人魚姫は叫びました。彼女の声は、浮かんでいるものたちと同じように聞こえました。それは天国のように美しすぎて、この世の音楽とは比べものにならないのでした。

The Little Mermaid

"To the daughters of the air," they answered; "a mermaid does not have an immortal soul, and can never have one unless she win's a man's love. Her after-life is decided by a power beyond her.

"The daughters of the air have no immortal souls either, but they can get one by their good acts.

"We fly to the hot countries where the heat and sickness destroy men's children. There we bring coolness and the smell of flowers to make people happy and healthy.

"After we have tried to do such good things for three hundred years, we can have an immortal soul like human beings. You, poor little mermaid, have tried to do good with all your heart. Like us, you have suffered and become a child of the air. Therefore, you too can win an immortal soul for yourself with three hundred years of good acts."

The little mermaid raised her bright arms to the sun. For the first time she felt tears in her eyes.

On board the ship a new day was beginning. She saw the Prince and his beautiful bride looking for her. They were watching the foam on the waves as if they knew she had jumped to her death.

■after-life 名来世 ■act 名行為 ■sickness 名病気 ■destroy 動殺す ■coolness 名涼しさ

人魚姫

「空気の娘たちのところへ」とそれは答えました。「人魚は不滅の魂をもっておらず、人間の愛を得なければ、けっして魂をもつことはできないのです。人魚の来世は、自分を超えた力によって決められるのです。

空気の娘たちも不滅の魂をもっていませんが、よい行いによって魂を得ることができます。
　私たちは熱と病気が人間の子どもたちをおびやかしている暑い国々へ飛んでいきます。そこへ私たちは涼しさと花の香りを届けて、人々を幸せにし、健康にするのです。
　そのようなよい行いをする努力を300年続けると、私たちは人間と同じように不滅の魂をもつことができます。かわいそうな小さな人魚姫よ、あなたは心をこめてよいことを行おうとしてきました。私たちと同じように、あなたは苦しんできたので、空気の子どもになったのです。ですから、あなたも300年よい行いをすれば、不滅の魂を得ることができるのですよ」
　小さな人魚姫は光り輝く腕を太陽の方へ上げました。生まれて初めて、目の中の涙を感じました。
　船の上では、新しい日が始まろうとしていました。人魚姫は、王子さまと美しい花嫁が、自分のことを探しているのを見ました。二人は、人魚姫が海に飛び込んで死んでしまったのをまるで知っているかのように、波にただよう泡を見ていました。

The Little Mermaid

Unseen by either of them, she kissed the bride's forehead and smiled upon the Prince. Then she rose with the other children of the air up to the clouds which were sailing the sky.

"For three hundred years we shall float and float and float. One day we will float right into God's kingdom."

"Yes, and we may get there still sooner," one said softly. "Unseen we enter the houses of men where there are children. When we find a good child who makes happy his parent's hearts, then God shortens the time of our efforts. The child does not know when we fly through the room; but when we smile with joy at such a child, a whole year is taken from the three hundred.

"But whenever we see a bad or mean child we cry tears of sadness. And every tear adds a day to our efforts!"

■unseen この世の　■equal 形目に見えない　■shorten 動短くする　■effort 名努力
■whenever 接 ～するときはいつでも　■mean 形意地悪な

人魚姫

　二人には見えない人魚姫は、花嫁のひたいにキスをし、王子さまにほほえみました。それから人魚姫は、他の空気の子どもたちといっしょに、空を流れる雲へと昇っていきました。

「300年の間、私たちは浮かんで浮かんで浮かび続け、そしていつか神さまの王国へたどり着くのですね」
「ええ、そして、そこにもう少し早く着けるかもしれません」と一人がやさしく言いました。「自分の姿を見られることなく、私たちは子どものいる人間の家へ入ります。両親の心を幸せにする、よい子どもを見つけると、神さまは私たちの努力すべき時間を短くしてくださいます。子どもは私たちが部屋に飛んできたことを知りません。けれども、私たちがそのような子どもに喜んでほほえむ時、300年からまるまる一年を減らしていただけるのです。
　ところが、悪い子や意地悪な子を見るたびに、私たちは悲しみの涙を流します。一粒の涙を流すとそのたびに、私たちの努力すべき300年に、もう一日が加えられることになるのです！」

覚えておきたい英語表現

> All day long they <u>used to</u> play in the palace's great room.
> （p. 10, 13行目）
> 一日中、彼らは宮殿の大きな部屋で遊んでいたものでした。

【解説】used to ～は、「（今はしないが）かつては、よく～したものだ」という昔の状態や習慣を表します。特に「現在は違うのだけれど」というニュアンスを表したいときに使います。

【例文】 I used to staying up late at night, but I often go to bed before 10 o'clock.
（かつては、夜遅くまで起きていたけど、いまは10時前に就寝する）

There used to be a convenience store at the corner, but there is a family restaurant.
（あの角には、かつてコンビニがあったが、いまはファミレスがある）

I used to work very hard, but I try not to do so.
（かつてはがむしゃらに働いたけど、いまはそうしないようにしている）

　used to ～に似た表現で、be used to ～ ing（～することに慣れている）という表現があります。be動詞がつくと ing形が用いられます。

I used to get up early. （かつては、早起きしたものだ）
I am used to getting up early. （早起きすることに慣れている）

> <u>It was</u> the youngest girl <u>who</u> wanted to know more than the others.（p. 16, 1行目）
> ほかのお姫さまたちのだれよりも、いろいろなことを知りたかったのは、一番若いお姫さまでした。

【解説】it is 〜 who ... は、強調構文といって、「…なのは、ほかならぬ〜だ」と It is と who で挟んだ部分を強調したい時に使われる表現です。挟まれたものが「人」なら who を使い、「もの」なら which を使います。That は、「人」でも、「もの」でも使うことができます。文全体が過去の話なら、is のかわりに was を使います。

【例文】　<u>It is</u> my father <u>who</u> cooks in my family.
　　　　（私の家庭では、料理するのは父だ）

　　　　<u>It was</u> in September <u>that</u> we met for the first time.
　　　　（私たちが最初に出会ったのは、9月でした）

　　　　<u>It is</u> the Internet <u>which</u> changed our life completely.
　　　　（私たちの生活を完璧に変えたのは、インターネットです）

The Emperor's New Clothes
裸の王さま

The Emperor's New Clothes

Many years ago, there lived an Emperor who loved new clothes. He spent most of his money on buying these fine, new clothes. He cared about nothing else, really. Not his army, not the arts, not even his people. No, he just liked to show off his new clothes. He had a different coat for every day of the year, and every hour of the day. In many countries, kings and emperors are busy with important matters. But this Emperor was usually busy changing his clothes.

The Emperor lived in a large, pleasant city. Every day, many strangers would come to the city for business or pleasure. One day, two men who said they were weavers arrived in the Emperor's city. They said they could weave the most beautiful and colorful clothes in the world.

■emperor 名皇帝　■care about ～を気に掛ける　■nothing else 他には何もない
■show off 見せびらかす　■matter 名事柄、問題　■stranger 名よそから来た人
■pleasure 名楽しみ　■weaver 名織り手

裸の王さま

　何年も前のこと、新しい洋服を愛する皇帝がいました。皇帝は、お金のほとんどを、美しく新しい服を買うために使いました。本当に、皇帝は他のことは何も気にかけなかったのでした。自分の軍隊、芸術、そして国民のことさえも気にかけなかったのです。そうです、皇帝は、自分の新しい洋服を見せびらかすことだけが好きだったのでした。皇帝は一年の間毎日、一時間ごとに別の上着に着がえました。多くの国では、王さまや皇帝は大事なお仕事で忙しいのですが、この皇帝は、いつも洋服を着がえるのに忙しいのでした。

　皇帝は、大きく、にぎやかな町に住んでいました。毎日、多くの人々が、仕事や遊びのためによそからその町を訪れました。ある日、自分たちを織り手だと名のる二人の男が、皇帝の町へやって来ました。二人は、自分たちはこの世でもっとも美しく華やかな服を織ることができる、と言いました。

The Emperor's New Clothes

They used only the finest material. They also said that the clothes they made were very, very special. These clothes could not be seen by foolish people or by people who were unfit for their jobs. However, nobody knew that these men were not really weavers. They were only pretenders.

When the Emperor heard of these men he was very interested. "These clothes would be of great value to me," thought the Emperor. "By wearing them I would know who was foolish and who was not. I would also know which of my ministers was unfit for his office. Yes, I want to wear some of that special cloth at once." He then gave the two men a lot of money in advance to begin their work.

So the men set up two weaving machines, called looms, and pretended to weave. But of course, there was nothing on the looms. They demanded the highest priced silk and gold materials. They put these materials in a safe place. Then they pretended to work on the empty looms until late at night.

■material 名材料、素材　■unfit 形不相応な　■pretender 名ふりをする人、詐称者
■value 名価値　■minister 名大臣　■at once すぐに　■set up 据え付ける
■weaving machine / loom 織り機　■pretend 動 〜のふりをする

裸の王さま

　二人は、最高の材料しか使いませんでした。彼らはまた、自分たちが仕立てる洋服はとても、とても特別なのだ、とも言いました。その洋服は、愚かな人や今の仕事に向いていない人には見ることができないのです。けれども、この二人が本当は織り手ではないということを、だれも知りませんでした。彼らは実は詐欺師だったのです。

　皇帝はこの二人のことを聞くと、とても興味をもちました。「そのような洋服は私にとってたいへん価値があるものであろう」と皇帝は考えました。「それを着れば、だれが愚か者でだれがそうでないか、わかるであろう。大臣の中で、だれが今の地位に向いていないかもわかるというものだ。そうだ、その特別な布でできた服をすぐに着たい」そして皇帝は二人に仕事を始めさせるために、前もって大金を渡しました。

　それから、その男たちは、織り機と呼ばれる、はた織り機を二台用意し、布を織るふりをしました。けれども、その織り機にはもちろん、何もかけられていなかったのです。二人は、もっとも高価な絹と金の材料を要求し、それを安全な場所に隠してしまいました。そして二人は、夜遅くまで何もない織り機に向かって働いているふりをしました。

The Emperor's New Clothes

"I wonder how my new clothes are coming along," thought the Emperor, after two days had passed. In his heart, he was a little afraid to visit the weavers. Because he remembered that foolish or unfit people could not see the cloth. Of course, he did not believe that he himself was foolish or unfit. He just thought it might be a good idea to send someone else first. "I will send my able old minister to check on the clothes," thought the Emperor. "For he is wise and surely fit for his office."

By now, most people in the city had heard of the wonderful new cloth. Everyone wanted to see how foolish or unfit their neighbors were. The old minister also knew of the cloth. When he walked into the room he saw the two men working at an empty loom. "Oh my!" he thought and opened his eyes very wide. "I can't see anything." But he was careful not to say so.

■wonder 動 ～を知りたいと思う　■come along 進行する　■It might be a good idea to ～した方がいいかもしれない　■able 形 能力［資格］のある　■Oh my! 何てことだ！

裸の王さま

「私の新しい服の進みぐあいはどうであろう」と皇帝は考えました。すでに二日がたっていました。心のうちでは、皇帝は、織り手のもとを訪れるのを少しおそれていました。愚かな人、今の仕事に向いていない人はその布を見ることができない、ということを覚えていたからです。もちろん、皇帝自身は、自分のことを愚かであるとか、今の地位にふさわしくないとは信じていませんでした。ただ、まずだれか他の者に様子を見に行かせる方がいいのではないかと考えただけです。「あの有能な老臣に服を見に行かせよう」と皇帝は考えました。「あの大臣はかしこい人間だし、もちろん今の地位にふさわしいのだから」

その頃には町のほとんどの人々が、そのすばらしい新しい服地の話を聞いていました。だれもが近所の人がどのくらい愚かなのか、どのくらい今の仕事に向いていないのかを知りたいのでした。老臣も、その服地について知っていました。老臣が部屋へ入った時、二人の男が何もない織り機に向かって働いているのが見えました。「なんということだ！」と彼は考え、目を大きく開けました。「私には何も見えないぞ」けれども彼は、注意深くそれを言わないようにしました。

The Emperor's New Clothes

The two pretenders asked him to come closer. They asked him if he thought the colors were beautiful. They pointed to the looms. The poor old minister looked hard but couldn't see a thing. Because there was nothing to see. "Oh my!" thought the minister. "Is it possible I am foolish? Or unfit for my office? I never thought so before. I surely can't tell the Emperor that I couldn't see anything."

"Well, what do you think?" asked one of the weavers.

"Oh, I've never seen more beautiful cloth! The most beautiful in the world!" said the old minister as he put on his glasses. "What patterns and colors! Yes, I'll tell the Emperor that I'm very pleased."

"Well, we're glad you like it," said the weavers. Then they told the minister the names of the colors and the patterns, so that the minister could tell the Emperor. And he did.

■point to 〜を指さす　■look hard まじまじと見る　■put on 〜を身に着ける
■glasses 名メガネ　■pattern 名模様

裸の王さま

　詐欺師の二人は、老臣にもっと近くまで来るようにと言いました。二人は老臣に、布の色は美しいと思うかと聞いて、織り機を指さしました。かわいそうな老臣は、よくよく見ましたが、何も見えませんでした。そこには、見えるものは何もなかったからです。「どうしたことだ！」と老臣は考えました。「私が愚か者だということだろうか？　それとも今の地位にふさわしくないということだろうか？　そんなことは今まで考えたことはなかったぞ。何も見えませんでした、などと皇帝にお伝えすることはけっしてできない」

　「それで、どう思われますか？」と織り手の一人が聞きました。

　「なんと、私はこれほど美しい布は見たことがない！　世界で一番美しい！」と、眼鏡をかけながら老臣が言いました。「なんとすばらしい模様と色であろう！　よし、皇帝に、私はたいへん満足したとお伝えしよう」

　「そうでございますか、気に入っていただけて光栄でございます」と織り手は言いました。そして二人は老臣に布の色と模様の名前を説明し、老臣がそれを皇帝に伝えられるようにしました。そして老臣は聞いたことを皇帝にお伝えしました。

The Emperor's New Clothes

The pretenders also asked for more money, more silk, and more gold. They needed the gold for weaving, they said. When they received these things they put them away in a safe place. Not one piece of material ever touched a loom. Still, they continued to weave on the empty looms.

A short time later the Emperor sent another able minister to see if his clothes were almost ready. This minister also looked and looked at the looms. But of course, there was nothing to see. "A pretty piece of cloth, don't you think?" asked the weavers. They pretended to show the patterns and colors to him.

"Surely I'm not foolish," thought the man. "Am I unfit for my job? Hmmm, is this a game? Well, I mustn't let anyone know I didn't see the cloth." And so he agreed with the weavers that the cloth was indeed beautiful. And that is what he told the Emperor.

Soon, everyone in town was talking about the wonderful cloth.

■put away しまい込む　■empty 形空の　■mustn't 助～してはいけない　■agree with（人）の意見に同意する

裸の王さま

　詐欺師の二人は、お金と絹と金がもっと必要だと求めました。布を織るために金が必要だと言うのです。与えられたものを受け取ると、それを隠してしまいました。織り機にかけられた材料は、まったくありませんでした。それでも、二人は何もない織り機に向かって織り続けました。

　それからまもなく、皇帝は別の有能な大臣に、自分の洋服が完成に近いかどうか見に行かせました。この大臣もまた、織り機を何度も何度も見ました。しかしもちろん、そこには見えるものは何もありませんでした。「美しい布だと思われませんか？」と織り手はたずねました。二人は布の模様と色を大臣に見せるふりをしました。

　「私はもちろん愚か者ではない」と大臣は考えました。「私は今の仕事に向いていないのだろうか？　ふーむ、これは何かの冗談なのか？　それにしても、私には布が見えなかったことはだれにも知られてはならないぞ」そういうわけで、大臣は、その布は本当に美しいと、織り手に同意しました。それから大臣は皇帝に、布がとても美しいことをお伝えしました。
　やがて、町のだれもがそのすばらしい布について話すようになりました。

The Emperor's New Clothes

🎧47 At this time the Emperor also wanted to see the cloth. So into the weaver's room he went. But he did not go alone. He went with many of the great people in his kingdom, including the two ministers.

"Just look at this lovely cloth, your Majesty," said the two ministers. Neither of them could see anything. However, both of them believed that all the others could see the cloth.

"What's wrong here?" thought the Emperor, for he could see nothing. "What happened to my sight? This is very bad. Could it be that I am foolish? Am I unfit to be Emperor? Oh, what shall I do?"

"Oh, it is very fine indeed," said the Emperor to the others. "I shall be quite happy to wear these clothes," he said smiling. The whole group of great men looked and looked; but they saw nothing either. "Yes, your Majesty, it is just fine," they all said to the Emperor. "The Grand Procession is coming soon," they also told him. "It would be a fine chance for you to wear these clothes for the first time."

■people 名臣下　■your Majesty〈呼び掛け〉陛下　■all the others その他の人たち
■sight 名視力、視覚　■grand 形盛大な、大～　■procession 名行列、行進

裸の王さま

　この頃には、皇帝もまた、その布を見たいと思いました。そうして、織り手の部屋へとおもむきました。けれども、一人では行きませんでした。王国の多くの優れた側近たちといっしょに行ったのです。その中には、あの二人の大臣も含まれていました。

　「この美しい布をご覧ください、陛下」と二人の大臣は言いました。二人とも、何も見えてはいませんでした。けれども二人とも、他の人々には布が見えているのだと信じていました。

　「いったいどうしたことだろう？」と皇帝は考えました。自分には何も見えなかったからです。「私の目に何が起こったのだろう？　これはとても困ったことだ。私が愚か者だということだろうか？　私は皇帝としてふさわしくないのだろうか？　ああ、どうしたらよいだろう？」

　「なんと、これは本当にすばらしい」と、皇帝は他の者たちに言いました。「その洋服を着ることをうれしく思うぞ」と、彼はほほえみながら言いました。皇帝といっしょに来た側近たちもみな、何度も何度も見ましたが、やはり何も見えませんでした。「はい、陛下、とてもすばらしいです」と、彼らはみな皇帝に言いました。そして「大行列がもうすぐございます」とも皇帝に言いました。「そのお洋服を初めてお召しになるよい機会となりましょう」

The Emperor's New Clothes

From mouth to mouth was heard, "Wonderful, beautiful, lovely." And the Emperor, thinking that everyone else could see the cloth, also seemed pleased. In fact, he gave the honor of "Weavers to the Emperor" to the two pretenders.

The evening before the Grand Procession was a busy one. The weavers stayed up all night working on the looms. People could see them pretending to make the cloth into clothes. At last they said, "There, the clothes are now ready!"

The Emperor, with his helpers, then came in. The weavers pretended to hold the clothes up in the air for all to see. "Look, your Majesty, here are the stockings, here are the pants, and here is the coat. This material is very, very light. When you wear it, it will feel as though you are not wearing anything. That is the beauty of the cloth."

"Of course!" said all the gentlemen. But they could see nothing, for there was nothing to see.

"And now, we would like to ask your Majesty to please take off his clothes," said the pretenders. "We will put on the new ones for you. In front of the large mirror, please! Thank you!"

■from mouth to mouth （うわさなどが）口から口へ　■honor 名称号　■stay up 寝ずに起きている　■pants 名ズボン

裸の王さま

「すばらしい、美しい、まったく美しい」と、人々の口から口へ伝わりました。そして皇帝も、家来たちにはその布が見えているらしいと考えたので、うれしそうにしていました。それどころか、皇帝は二人のペテン師に「皇帝ご指名の織り手」という名誉を与えたのでした。

大行列の前夜は忙しいものでした。二人の織り手は、一晩中織り機に向かって働いていました。人々は二人が布を洋服に仕立て上げているふりをしているのを見ることができました。ついに二人は言いました。「これだ、洋服が完成したぞ！」

それから皇帝が、おつきの者たちとともに部屋に入ってきました。二人の織り手は、みんなに見えるように洋服を空中に持ち上げるふりをしました。「ご覧ください、陛下。こちらが靴下、こちらがズボン、そしてこちらが上着でございます。この素材はとてもとても軽いものでございます。これをお召しになっても、まるで何もお召しになっていらっしゃらないようにお感じになるでしょう。それこそが、この布のすばらしいところなのでございます」

「なるほど！」と、すべての人々が言いました。けれども、みんな、何も見えませんでした。そこには見えるものは何もなかったからです。

「さていよいよ、陛下におかれましては、お洋服を脱いでいただけますようお願いいたします」と二人の詐欺師は言いました。「私どもが新しい洋服をお着せいたします。どうぞ、この大きい鏡の前までおいでくださいませ！　ありがとうございます！」

The Emperor's New Clothes

The weavers pretended to dress the Emperor in his new clothes, piece by piece. They tied this and that, pulled here and there. The Emperor turned and looked at himself in the mirror.

"What a wonderful suit it is! How nicely it fits!" cried all the people at once. "What colors! What patterns! How lovely!"

"All right, I am quite ready for the Grand Procession," said the Emperor. He looked in the mirror one last time. "Does everything fit perfectly? Let us go on." The helpers then picked up the tail of the long coat and held their hands in the air. They didn't want others to know they could see nothing.

And so, the group marched outside to begin the procession. Everyone watching from the streets and the windows said, "My, what beautiful clothes the Emperor is wearing! How perfectly they fit!" Of course, no one wanted others to know that he could see no clothes. They might think him foolish or unfit for his position. In fact, the Emperor had never received nicer words about any of his clothes.

■piece by piece 一つ一つ　■suit 名 スーツ、一組の衣服　■one last time 最後にもう一度　■helper 名 おつきの者　■march 動 行進する

裸の王さま

　織り手たちは、一枚ずつ、皇帝に新しい洋服を着せるふりをしました。二人はいろいろな部分を結んだり、あちこちひっぱったりしました。皇帝は振り返り、鏡に映る自分を見ました。

「なんとすばらしいスーツでしょう！　陛下のお体になんとぴったりと合っていらっしゃることでしょう！」すべての人が同時に叫びました。「なんという色！　なんという模様！　なんとすばらしい！」
「よろしい、大行列へ行く用意はしっかりできておるぞ」と皇帝は言いました。皇帝は鏡を最後にもう一度見ました。「ぜんぶぴったりと合っているだろうか？　それでは行こう」そしておつきの者たちは、上着の長いすそを持ち上げ、彼らの手を空中に持ち上げました。自分には何も見えないことを他の人たちに知られたくなかったのです。

　そうして、皇帝の一隊は外へ出て、大行列を始めました。通りや窓から見ていた人々はみな、こう言いました。「ああ、なんて美しい洋服を皇帝はお召しになっているのでしょう！　なんてよくお似合いなんでしょう！」もちろん、だれもがみんな、自分には洋服が見えないことを他の人に知られたくなかったのでした。自分のことを愚か者とか、今の地位にふさわしくないと思われてしまうかもしれないからです。実際、皇帝はほかのどの服のときでも、この新しい服ほどほめられたことはありませんでした。

The Emperor's New Clothes

 Suddenly, a small child in the crowd cried, "Why, he's got nothing on!"

"Listen to the true words of a child," said the father. Soon, everyone was talking with his neighbor about what the child said. "He has nothing on! There is a child who says he's wearing nothing."

Finally, the whole crowd cried, "He really has nothing on!"

At that point, the Emperor heard the crowd and he knew they were right. He felt very foolish. But at the same time he thought, "I must continue with this procession until the end." So he tried to pretend that nothing was wrong and just kept marching. While behind him, his helpers continued to hold up the long coat that wasn't there.

■suddenly 副 突然に ■crowd 名 群衆 ■get on 身に着ける ■at that point その時点で ■nothing is wrong 少しもおかしくない ■hold up 持ち上げる

裸の王さま

　突然、群衆の中にいた小さな子どもが叫びました。「あれ、あの人は何も着てないよ！」
　「子どもが本当のことを言っているのを聞け」とその子の父親が言いました。みんなはすぐに、子どもが言ったことを近所の人と話し始めました。「皇帝は何も着ていないぞ！　皇帝は何も着ていないと言っている子どもがいるんだ」
　とうとう、人々はみな叫びました。「皇帝は何も着ていない！」

　その時、皇帝には人々の叫びが聞こえましたし、自分でも彼らが正しいことがわかっていました。皇帝は自分のことをひどく愚かに感じました。けれどもまた、彼は考えました。「私はこの行列を最後まで続けなければならない」そして皇帝は何も問題がないようにふるまい、行進を続けました。その後ろでは、おつきの者たちが、そこにはないはずの長い上着のすそを持ち上げ続けていました。

| 覚えておきたい英語表現 |

> <u>I wonder how</u> my new clothes are coming along. （p. 98, 1行目）
> 私の新しい服の進みぐあいはどうであろう。

【解説】I wonderのあとに、疑問文を続けると、「～かしら」とか「～はどうかな」という意味を表します。Yes/Noで答えられるふつうの疑問文は ～の部分にif か whether をつけて、〈主語＋動詞～〉の語順になります。WhatやHowなどで始まる疑問文は、何もつけず、〈主語＋動詞～〉の語順にします。

【例文】　I wonder if this water is good for drinking.
　　　　（この水、飲めるのかなあ）

　　　　I wonder whether Mr. Kato will come to our wedding?
　　　　（加藤さんは、私たちの結婚式にくるかしら）

　　　　I wonder how tall is the Tokyo Skytree?
　　　　（スカイツリーの高さはどのくらいかな）

　　　　I have been wondering where Chris is from?
　　　　（クリスはどこの出身かな）

> **What a wonderful suit it is!**（p. 108, 5行目）
> なんてすばらしいスーツなんでしょう！
>
> **How nicely it fits!**（p. 108, 5行目）
> なんて、体にぴったりと合っているのでしょう。

【解説】「なんて～なんだろう！」という意味を表す「感嘆文」には、2通りの言い方があります。違いは、「名詞」があるかどうかだけです。まず、語順を確認しましょう。Whatには名詞が伴います。したがって、aやanも現れます。

　　　　Whatの場合：What + a（an）+ 形容詞 + 名詞 + 主語 + 動詞！
　　　　Howの場合 ：How + 形容詞または副詞 + 主語 + 動詞！

感嘆文の場合、あまりにも感動が大きい場合、主語と動詞は省略されます。

【例文】　What a wonderful night!
　　　　（なんてすてきな夜なんだろう）

　　　　 How lovely!
　　　　（なんてかわいいんだろう）

　　　　What an easy question this is!
　　　　（これはなんと易しい問題なんだろう）

　　　　How easy this question is!
　　　　（この問題はなんと易しいのでしょう）

　　　　What a beautiful planet our Earth is!
　　　　（なんと美しいんでしょう、私たちの地球は）

　　　　What colors!
　　　　（まあ、なんという色なんでしょう）

　　　　colorsと複数形なので、aもanもなし。また感動のあまり、形容詞も省略されている。

The Steadfast Tin Soldier
すずの兵隊

The Steadfast Tin Soldier

There were once twenty-five tin soldiers. All of them were brothers because they had all been made from the same kitchen spoon. They shouldered long guns and looked straight ahead. Indeed, they looked very smart in their red and blue uniforms. "Tin soldiers!" That was the first thing they heard when the little boy took the top off their box. The boy was very happy because he had received them as a birthday present. He took them out of the box and put them on the table. Each soldier looked just like the next—except for one, which had only a single leg; he was the last one to be made, and there wasn't quite enough tin left. Yet he stood just as well on his one leg as the others did on their two; and he is the hero of this story.

■once 副あるとき　■tin 名スズ（錫）　■made from （原料）でできている
■shoulder 動担ぐ　■look straight ahead 真っすぐ前を見る　■smart 形利口な
■take the top off 蓋を取る　■take ~ out of ～を…から取り出す　■except for ～を除けば

すずの兵隊

　むかし、25人のすずの兵隊がいました。みんな同じ大型スプーンからつくられた兄弟でした。兵隊は、長い銃を肩にかつぎ、まっすぐ前を向いていました。赤と青の制服を着ていて、本当に利口そうに見えました。「すずの兵隊だ！」それは、兵隊が最初に聞いたことでした。小さい男の子が彼らの入っている箱のふたを開けた時にそう言ったのです。小さい男の子は、兵隊をお誕生日のプレゼントとしてもらったので、とても幸せでした。男の子は兵隊を箱から出し、テーブルの上へ置きました。どの兵隊もみんな同じように見えました。ただし、一つだけちがっていました。その兵隊には足が一本しかなかったのでした。その兵隊は最後につくられたので、すずがもうあまり残っていなかったのです。それでも、彼は二本足の兵隊たちと同じように、一本足でちゃんと立っていました。そして、彼がこのお話の主役なのです。

The Steadfast Tin Soldier

There were many other toys on the table, but the first one everyone noticed was a paper castle. Through its little windows you could see into the little rooms. In front of the castle were very small trees. They stood around a piece of glass which was meant to be a lake. Beautiful white birds sat on the lake. The whole scene was like a dream; and the prettiest thing of all was a girl who stood in the open doorway. She too was cut out of paper; but her skirt was of the finest cotton. A blue ribbon crossed her shoulder and was held by a large, shiny, glass diamond. This lovely little girl held both her arms up high, for she was a dancer. In fact, one of her legs was raised so high in the air that the tin soldier could not see it at all. He thought that she too had only one leg.

■be meant to be ～であることを意図としている　■lake 名湖　■doorway 名戸口
■be cut out of paper 紙から切り抜かれている　■skirt 名スカート　■hold ~ up high ～を高くかざす　■in the air 空中に

すずの兵隊

　テーブルの上にはほかにもたくさんのおもちゃがありましたが、みんなが最初に気がついたのは、紙でできたお城でした。小さな窓から、中の小さい部屋をのぞきこむことができました。お城の前には、とても小さな木がありました。それらは湖のつもりで置かれた鏡を囲んで立っていました。美しい白鳥が湖にいました。すべての光景はまるで夢のようでした。その中でも一番美しいものは、開いた出入口に立っている少女でした。少女も紙から切り抜かれたものでしたが、スカートは上等な綿の布でできていました。青いリボンが肩からかけられ、大きなきらきらしたガラスのダイヤモンドで留められていました。この美しい少女は、両腕を高く上げていました。踊り子だったからです。そのため、彼女の片足はとても高く上げられていたので、一本足のすずの兵隊には、それはまったく見えませんでした。彼は、少女も一本足なのだと思いました。

The Steadfast Tin Soldier

"Oh she would be the perfect wife for me," he thought. "But she is so pretty. She lives in a castle, and I have only a box; and there are twenty-five of us in that! Surely there isn't room for her. Still, I can get to know her." So he lay down behind a tobacco box on the table where he could easily watch the little paper dancer. She continued to stand on one leg without falling down.

When evening came, all the other tin soldiers were put in their box, and the children went to bed. Now the toys began to play on their own. They played at visiting, going to school, having battles, and going to parties. The tin soldiers made noises in their box because they also wanted to play. But they couldn't get the top off their box. The nutcracker moved in circles, the pencil wrote on the paper; there was so much movement and talking that the yellow bird also began to sing. The only two who didn't move were the tin soldier and the little dancer. She continued to stand on the point of her foot, with her arms held out; he stood very still on his single leg—always watching her.

■get to know 〜と知り合いになる ■lay 動lie（横になる）の過去形 ■tobacco 名刻みたばこ ■fall down 転ぶ ■go to bed 就寝する ■get off 〜を外す ■on one's own 自力で ■nutcracker 名くるみ割り人形

すずの兵隊

　「ああ、彼女ならぼくの奥さんにぴったりだろう」と兵隊は考えました。「でも、あの娘は美しすぎる。彼女はお城に住んでいるけれど、ぼくが住んでいるのはただの箱。しかもその中に25人も住んでいるんだ！　もちろん彼女には狭すぎる。でも、ぼくはあの娘と知り合いになることはできるぞ」そのために、兵隊はテーブルの上に置かれたたばこの箱の後ろに横になりました。そこからは小さな紙の踊り子を見ることができました。踊り子は倒れもせずに、あいかわらず一本足で立っていました。

　夜になると、他のすずの兵隊はみんな箱に入れられ、子どもたちはベッドに入りました。さあ、今こそ、おもちゃたちは自分たちだけで遊び始めました。お客さんごっこ、学校ごっこ、戦争をしたり、パーティーに行ったりしました。すずの兵隊たちも遊びたかったので、箱の中で音を立てました。けれども、箱のふたをはずすことはできませんでした。くるみ割り人形がくるくると回り、鉛筆は紙の上に字を書きました。みんなが動きまわり、おしゃべりをしていたので、黄色い鳥も歌い始めました。動かなかったのは、一本足のすずの兵隊と小さい踊り子だけでした。踊り子はつま先で立ち続け、腕は伸ばしたままでした。兵隊は、ずっと彼女を見続けながら、一本足でじっと立っていました。

The Steadfast Tin Soldier

Then the clock struck twelve midnight. Suddenly, the top flew off the tobacco box and up came a little black jack-in-the-box. There was no tobacco in the box—it was just a toy.

"Tin soldier!" cried the jack-in-the-box. "Keep your eyes to yourself!"

But the tin soldier seemed not to hear.

"All right, just you wait till tomorrow!" said the unkind jack-in-the-box.

When morning came and the children returned, the tin soldier was placed next to the window. Then something happened—it may have been the jack-in-the-box or just the wind blowing, but suddenly the window opened up and out fell the tin soldier. He fell three floors down to the ground. It was a very bad fall! His leg pointed up, and his head pointed down. Also, his long gun was stuck in a space between the stones.

■struck 動strike(〈時を〉打つ)の過去形　■jack-in-the-box 名びっくり箱　■unkind 形不親切な　■be stuck in ～にはまり込んでいる

すずの兵隊

　やがて時計が午前零時を告げました。突然たばこの箱のふたが飛んで、びっくり箱の小さな黒いピエロが飛び出してきました。箱の中にたばこはなく、ただのおもちゃなのでした。

「すずの兵隊さん！」と、ピエロは叫びました。「ジロジロ見るのはおやめなさい！」
　けれども、すずの兵隊には聞こえないようでした。
「そうかい、それなら明日何が起こるか待ってろよ！」と意地の悪いピエロは言いました。
　朝が来て子どもたちがもどってくると、すずの兵隊は窓のそばに置かれました。すると何かが起こりました。それはピエロが起こしたことかも、あるいはただ風が吹いたからだけかもしれませんが、突然窓が開き、すずの兵隊は窓から落ちてしまいました。兵隊は三階から地面に落ちました。それはひどい落ち方でした！　彼の脚は上を向き、頭は下になりました。また、彼の長い銃は、石と石の間にはさまってしまいました。

The Steadfast Tin Soldier

The little boy and his sister went to look for him in the street. Although they almost walked on him, they could not see him. If he had called out, "Here I am!" they would have found him easily. But the tin soldier didn't think that was the right thing to do when he was in uniform.

Now it began to rain; the drops fell fast and heavy. When it was over, a pair of boys passed by. "Look!" said one of them. "There's a tin soldier. Let's put him out to sea."

So they made a little paper boat and put the tin soldier in the middle. Then they put the boat in the water which was running down the street. Away he went, and the two boys ran beside him shouting happily. My, how fast the water ran, and how big the waves! It had been a hard rain. The paper boat moved up and down, round and round. The soldier felt light-headed. But he was as steadfast as ever, not moving at all, still looking straight ahead and holding his long gun.

■walk on 〜の上を歩く ■call out 叫ぶ ■My 間 おやまあ ■round and round グルグルと ■light-headed 形 目まいがするような ■steadfast 形（意志などが）確固たる、不動の

すずの兵隊

　小さな男の子とその姉が、兵隊を街路まで探しに来ました。子どもたちはもう少しで彼を踏みつけそうになりましたが、彼のことは見えませんでした。もし彼が「ぼくはここにいますよ！」と叫んでいたら、簡単に見つけてもらうことができたでしょう。けれども、すずの兵隊は、自分が制服を着ている時は、それは正しい行いではないと思いました。

　雨が降り始めました。雨粒が速く激しく落ちてきました。雨がやんだ時、二人の男の子が通りかかりました。「見て！」と一人の子が言いました。「あそこにすずの兵隊がいるぞ。あいつを海まで流してやろう」

　そして二人は小さな紙のボートをつくり、すずの兵隊をまん中に乗せました。それから、ボートを道に流れている溝の水に浮かべました。すぐに兵隊は流されていき、二人の少年は楽しそうに叫びながら、その横を走っていきました。ああ、水の流れはなんと速く、そして波はなんと高かったことでしょう！　激しい雨が降ったあとだったからです。紙のボートは上下に揺れ、グルグルと回りました。すずの兵隊は頭がふらふらとしました。けれども、今までにも増してまっすぐの姿勢で、まったく動かず、前を向き、長い銃をかついだままでした。

The Steadfast Tin Soldier

Suddenly, the boat entered a dark tunnel under the street. Yes, it was as dark as the box at home. "Wherever am I going now?" the tin soldier wondered. "No, I don't like this at all. Ah! If only the young dancer were here in the boat with me. I wouldn't care if it was even darker."

Just then, from its home in the tunnel, jumped a large water-rat. "Do you have a passport?" it asked. "No entry without a passport!"

But the tin soldier never said a word; he only held his gun closer. The boat moved on quickly, with the rat running behind. Ugh! How angry the rat was, and shouted, "Stop him! Stop him! He hasn't paid his money! He hasn't shown his passport!"

There was no stopping the boat, though. The water ran stronger and stronger. The tin soldier could just see a little daylight far ahead. But at the same time he heard a loud rushing noise. A less steadfast man would have been afraid. Just think! Soon, the underground stream would drop like a great waterfall into a bigger stream.

■if only ただ〜でさえあればいいのだが ■water-rat 名水生ネズミ ■entry 名入ること ■shown 動show（見せる）の過去分詞形 ■daylight 名日光 ■ahead 副前方に ■rushing noise （サーッ・ザーッなどの）激しいノイズ ■less 副より少なく《littleの比較級》 ■waterfall 名滝

すずの兵隊

　突然、ボートは街路の下にある暗いトンネルに入りました。そう、それは家にある箱と同じくらい暗かったのです。「ぼくは今いったいどこへ向かっているんだろう？」とすずの兵隊は思いました。「いや、これはひどいことになってしまった。ああ！　あの若い踊り子がこのボートにぼくといっしょにいてくれたらなあ。そうしたら、もっと暗くても気にならないだろうに」

　ちょうどその時、トンネルにある自分の家から、大きな水生ネズミが飛び出してきました。「おまえさんは通行証をもっているかい？」と水生ネズミは聞きました。「通行証がなけりゃ、通してやらないぞ！」

　けれども、すずの兵隊は一言もしゃべりませんでした。彼は銃をもっと自分の体の近くにかつぎ直しただけでした。ボートはものすごい速さで前へ進み、水生ネズミはその後ろを走っていました。ああ！　水生ネズミはどんなにひどく怒っていたことでしょう。そしてこう叫びました。「ヤツを止めろ！　ヤツを止めろ！　あいつは金を払っていないんだ！　通行証を見せていないんだ！」

　けれども、ボートを止めることはできないのでした。水の流れはますます激しくなりました。すずの兵隊は、ずっと先の方にほんの少しだけ日の光を見ることができました。しかし同時に、ザーッという激しい音が聞こえてきました。彼ほどしっかりしていない人だったら、とても怖かったことでしょう。考えてもみてください！　地下の流れはもうすぐ、もっと大きな流れの中に、まるで大きな滝のように落ちて行くのです。

The Steadfast Tin Soldier

But how could he stop! It was too late. The boat raced on, and the poor tin soldier tried to be strong. No one could say that he was afraid.

Suddenly the little boat went round three or four times, then filled with water. The tin soldier stood in water up to his neck. Deeper and deeper went the boat; softer and softer became the paper. At last the water closed over the soldier's head. He thought of the lovely little dancer whom he would never see again. In his ears rang the words of a song:

"Onward, onward, warrior brave! Fear not danger, nor the grave." Then the boat came undone and out fell the tin soldier. He was quickly eaten by a fish.

Oh, how dark it was inside the fish! Even darker than before, and much less space to move. But the tin soldier had no fear. He was as steadfast as ever, his long gun still at his shoulder. The fish began to move and turn wildly, and then became quite still. Something bright passed by quickly—then all around was welcome daylight. A voice cried out, "The tin soldier!"

■race on 高速で動き続ける ■onward 副前方へ ■warrior 名戦士 ■brave 形勇敢な ■grave 名墓 ■come undone ほどける ■wildly 副乱暴に

すずの兵隊

　けれど、彼にどうやってそれを止めることができたでしょう！　もう遅すぎました。ボートは疾走し続け、かわいそうなすずの兵隊は強くあろうとしました。彼が怖がっているとはだれも言えないでしょう。

　突然、その小さなボートは三、四回くるくると回ると、水が入ってきました。すずの兵隊は首まで水につかりながら立っていました。ボートは深く、さらに深く沈んでいき、紙はもっともっと柔らかくなってきました。とうとう水は兵隊の頭の上まできてしまいました。兵隊はもう二度と会うことはない美しい小さな踊り子のことを考えました。耳の中にある歌詞が聞こえてきました。

　「進め、進め、勇敢な兵隊よ！　危険も墓もおそれるな」それからボートは壊れ、すずの兵隊はボートから落ちたかと思うと、すぐに魚に食べられてしまいました。

　ああ、魚の体の中はなんと暗かったことでしょう！　前よりももっと暗く、動ける空間はもっと少ないのでした。しかし、すずの兵隊はおそれていませんでした。今まで以上にしっかりと立ち、長い銃はまだ肩にありました。魚は動き始め、大きくひっくり返り、そしてぜんぜん動かなくなりました。何か輝くものが素早く通り過ぎ、それからまわりはぜんぶ、うれしい日の光でいっぱいになりました。叫び声が聞こえました。「あのすずの兵隊だ！」

The Steadfast Tin Soldier

The fish had been caught, taken to market, sold and carried into the kitchen where the cook had cut it open. Now she picked up the soldier, holding him with her fingers. She took him into the living room so that all the family could see. Truly, they were surprised. But the tin soldier was not at all proud. They stood him up on the table. And there—well, the world is full of wonders—he saw that he was in the same room where his journey had started. There were the very same children; there were the very same toys; there was the fine paper castle with the lovely little dancer at the door. She still stood on one leg, with the other raised high in the air. Ah, she was steadfast too. The tin soldier's heart was moved. If he had not been a soldier he might have started to cry. He looked at her, and she looked at him. But not a word was spoken.

And then a strange thing happened. One of the small boys picked up the tin soldier and threw him into the oven. He had no reason for doing this; maybe the unkind jack-in-the-box made him do it.

■truly 副本当に　■journey 名旅　■wonder 名感嘆すべきこと　■very same まさにその　■reason 名理由　■make someone do（人）に〜させる

すずの兵隊

　兵隊を飲み込んだ魚は捕まえられ、市場へ持っていかれて売られたあとで、キッチンに運ばれ、そこで料理人にその腹を切り開かれたのでした。料理人は兵隊を拾いあげ、指でつかんでいました。彼女は兵隊を、家族全員が見られるように居間へ持っていきました。彼らは本当に驚きました。しかし、すずの兵隊は、自分のことを誇りにはまったく思っていませんでした。みんなは兵隊をテーブルの上に立たせました。そしてそこで——まあ、この世は驚きに満ち満ちているものです——兵隊は自分が、元々の旅が始まったのと同じ部屋にいるのがわかったのです。そこには前と同じ子どもたちがいました。前とまったく同じおもちゃがありました。ドアのところに美しい小さな踊り子がいる、りっぱな紙のお城もありました。踊り子はまだ一本足で立っていて、もう一本の足は宙に高く上げられていました。ああ、彼女も動かないままだったのです。すずの兵隊は感動しました。もし自分が兵隊ではなかったら、泣き出していたかもしれません。兵隊は踊り子を見、踊り子も兵隊を見ました。しかし二人とも何も言いませんでした。

　それから不思議なことが起こりました。少年の一人がすずの兵隊をつかみ、かまどに投げ込んだのです。その子には、そんなことをする理由は何もなかったのです。もしかしたら、あの意地悪なびっくり箱のピエロが、彼にそうさせたのかもしれません。

The Steadfast Tin Soldier

The tin soldier stood in a bright light. The heat was strong. But he didn't know if it was because of the fire, or his burning love. His bright colors were now gone—but if it was because of his journey, or his sadness, no one knew. He looked at the pretty little dancer, and she looked at him. He felt that he was melting away, but he still stood steadfast, holding his gun. Suddenly the door flew open, and a rush of air caught the little paper girl. She flew right into the oven, straight to the waiting tin soldier. There she quickly caught fire and disappeared.

Soon after, the soldier had melted down to a small piece of tin. The next day, when the cook cleaned the oven, she found him. He was in the form of a little tin heart. And the dancer? All they found was her glass diamond, and that was as black as night.

■melt away 溶けてなくなる　■fly open パッと開く　■melt down 溶ける

すずの兵隊

　すずの兵隊はまぶしい光の中に立っていました。かまどの中の熱は強いものでした。けれども兵隊は、それが火によるものなのか、それとも彼の燃えさかるような愛によるものなのか、わかりませんでした。兵隊の体の鮮やかな色はもうなくなってしまいました。しかし、それが旅によるものなのか、または悲しみによるものなのか、だれにもわかりませんでした。兵隊はきれいな小さな踊り子を見て、踊り子も兵隊を見ました。兵隊は自分が溶けていくのを感じましたが、それでもそのまま不動のままで、銃をかついで立っていました。突然ドアが開き、一陣の風が小さな紙の踊り子をとらえました。踊り子はかまどの中に飛び込み、そこで待っていたすずの兵隊のところへまっすぐに来ました。そこで踊り子の体にすぐ火がつき、彼女は消えてしまいました。

　その後すぐに兵隊は溶けて、小さなすずのかたまりになりました。次の日、料理人がかまどの掃除をした時、彼女は兵隊を見つけました。それは小さなハート形のすずのかたまりになっていました。そして踊り子はどうなったでしょうか？　みんなが見つけることができたのは、踊り子のガラスのダイヤモンドだけでした。それは、夜と同じくらいまっ黒になっていました。

> 覚えておきたい英語表現

> She continued to stand on the point of her foot, <u>with her arms held out</u>. (p. 120, 下から3行目)
> 彼女は、つま先で立ち続け、腕は伸ばしたままでした。

【解説】この文の下線部は「〜しながら」という意味を表す「付帯状況のwith」と言われるものです。〈with + 名詞 + 状態を表すことば〉という語順です。状態を表すことばには、形容詞、動詞のing形、過去分詞、前置詞句などがあります。

【例文】　Don't speak with your mouth full.
　　　　（口をいっぱいにして、話をするな）

　　　　My mother listened to music with her eyes closed.
　　　　（母は、目を閉じながら、音楽を聴いていた）

　　　　My friends are standing with tears running on their cheeks.
　　　　（私の友人たちは、ほほに涙を流しながら、立っていました）

　　　　Please decorate the cake with this candle in the middle.
　　　　（このろうそくを真ん中にして、ケーキを飾ってください）

> I wouldn't care if it was even darker. (p. 126, 5行目)
> もっと暗かったとしても、私は気にならないだろう。

【解説】「仮定法」の表現です。仮定法は、難しく考えないようにしましょう。基本は、現在のことをいうときには『過去形』、過去のことを言うときは『大過去（had + 過去分詞）』（つまり過去完了形）を使うのです。「現在が過去、過去が大過去」と覚えておきましょう。またwasのかわりにwereを使います。

【例文】 If it was (were) snowing now, I would stay home today.
（もしいま雪が降っているならば、私は今日は家にいます）

If my grandpa were better, I would talk to him more.
（もし祖父が元気ならば、私はもっと祖父と話をしたい）

If I were you, I would not say such a thing.
（もし私があなただったら、私はそんなことを言わないでしょう）

If you had been there, our presentation would have been successful.
（もし君がそこにいたならば、私たちのプレゼンはうまくいったのになあ）

The Ugly Duckling
みにくいアヒルの子

The Ugly Duckling

It was so pretty out in the country in the summertime.

The fields were full of tall, yellow corn. The wheat was turning gold. All around the fields were great, green forests and deep blue lakes. In the trees, birds were speaking many different languages to each other. Yes, it was very nice in the country.

The sun was shining on an old country house that stood near a pond. From the walls down to the water grew high plants with wide leaves. Under these leaves a mother duck lay upon her eggs in her nest. By this time she had become a little tired and lonely. She had few visitors; the other ducks enjoyed swimming in the water more than sitting and talking with her.

Finally, one egg began to break open, then another and another. The little eggs had come alive. "Peep! Peep!" was the cry from the heads that now appeared.

■summertime 名夏季　■corn 名トウモロコシ　■wheat 名小麦　■pond 名池　■nest 名巣　■visitor 名訪問者　■come alive 活気づく　■appear 動現れる

みにくいアヒルの子

　いなかの夏はとても美しいのでした。
　畑には高く育った黄色いトウモロコシがたくさんありました。小麦は金色になっていくところでした。畑のまわりはすべて、大きな緑の森や深く青い湖に囲まれていました。木々の間で、鳥たちがいろいろな言葉で互いにおしゃべりをしていました。本当に、いなかはとてもよいところでした。
　太陽が、池の近くにある古い大きな家を照らしていました。その家の塀から池までは、葉っぱが大きく、背が高い植物が生えていました。その葉っぱの下で、お母さんアヒルは、巣の中で卵をあたためていました。その頃、お母さんは少し疲れてきていて、寂しい思いをつのらせていました。顔を見せに来てくれる仲間はほとんどいませんでした。他のアヒルは、彼女のところで座って話をしているよりも、水の中で泳いでいる方が楽しかったからでした。
　やっと一つの卵が、そしてもう一つ、またさらに一つの卵が割れはじめました。卵からヒナがかえったのです。「ピー！　ピー！」と、卵からもう頭をのぞかせたヒナたちが鳴きました。

The Ugly Duckling

The mother duck welcomed them into the world. "Quick! Quick!" she told them, "Look around." So they all ran about under the green, green leaves looking here and there. Their mother watched them happily.

"How big the world is!" said the young ducklings. True, there had been very little room inside the eggs.

"Do you think that this is the whole world?" asked their mother. "Why, the world goes beyond this garden and the next, right into the farmer's field; but I have never been there. Well, I guess all of you are out." She stood up and saw that there was one more egg to go. "Oh, the biggest egg is still lying there. How much longer do I have to wait for it? I'm sick and tired of it!" And down she sat again.

"Well, how are things with you?" asked an old duck who came to pay her a visit.

"This last egg is taking such a long time!" answered the sitting duck. "It's not ready to come out yet! But look at the others! Aren't they pretty little ducklings? They look just like their father, the playboy! He never comes to see me!"

■look around 周りを見回す　■run about 走り回る　■duckling 名アヒルの子
■one more ~ to go もう１つ〜が残っている　■sick and tired of 〜にはうんざりである　■pay ~ a visit 〜を訪問する　■playboy プレイボーイ、遊び人

みにくいアヒルの子

　お母さんはヒナの誕生を喜んで迎えました。「早く！　早く！」と彼女はヒナたちに言いました。「まわりを見てごらん」それからヒナたちは、濃い緑の葉っぱの下を走りまわり、あちこち見てまわりました。お母さんは、幸せそうにヒナを見守っていました。
　「世界って、なんて大きいんだろう！」と、ヒナが言いました。そう感じたのも当然です。卵の中はとても狭かったからです。
　「これが世界のすべてだと思うかい？」とお母さんは聞きました。「なんと、世界はこの庭やとなりの庭より先の農家の畑まで続いているのよ。私はそこまで行ったことはないけれど。さて、みんな卵から出てきたようね」彼女は立ち上がると、もう一つ卵が残っているのを見つけました。「まあ、一番大きな卵がまだあそこにあるわ。あとどのくらい待たなきゃいけないのかしら？　もう本当にうんざりだわ！」そしてお母さんはまた座りました。
　「さて、おまえさん、どうしてるかね？」と、彼女を訪ねてきた年寄りのアヒルが聞きました。
　「この最後の卵はすごく時間がかかっているんですよ！」と座っているお母さんは答えました。「この子はまだ卵から出てくる準備ができていないんです！　でも、他の子たちを見てください！　小さくてかわいい子たちでしょう？　父親にまさにそっくりなんです。プレイボーイですけどね！　私にぜんぜん会いに来てくれないんですから！」

The Ugly Duckling

"Let me see the egg that won't open up!" said the old duck. "Believe me, it's a turkey egg. I was fooled like that myself once. What trouble those young ones were, too! They were afraid of the water. Just wouldn't go in. I tried to talk them in at first, then I tried pushing them. But it was no use. Yes, I say it's a turkey egg. Leave it alone and go teach the other children to swim!"

"No, I should sit on it a little longer," said the mother. "I've sat so long already, a few more hours won't hurt."

"As you like!" said the old duck, and she walked ducklike back to the water.

At last the big egg began to break open. "Peep! Peep!" said the baby duck as it tried to shake itself out of the egg. He was so big and ugly. The mother looked at him.

"What an ugly duckling it is!" she cried. "He doesn't look like any of the others. Surely, it can't be a turkey! Well, we'll soon find out! Into the water he goes, even if I have to push him!"

■turkey 图七面鳥　■no use 全く役に立たない　■as you like あなたの好きなように
■-like 尾〜のような　■shake oneself out of 〜から自身を脱け出させる　■find out 明らかにする

みにくいアヒルの子

「まだ割れようとしない卵を見せてごらん！」と年寄りのアヒルが言いました。「信じられないかもしれないが、これは七面鳥の卵だね。あたしもむかし、だまされたことがあるのさ。あの子たちにはひどく手を焼いたもんだ！ 七面鳥は水が怖いんだ。水にぜんぜん入っていこうとしなかった。あたしは、初めはあの子たちをなだめすかして、それから強要してもみた。でも、無駄だったね。そうそう、それは七面鳥の卵だと言っているんだ。そいつは放っておいて、他の子たちに泳ぎを教えに行きなさい！」

「いいえ、もう少しだけこの卵の上に座っています」とお母さんは言いました。「今まで長いあいだ座っていたんですから、あと何時間かそうしていてもかまいません」

「勝手にするがいいさ！」と年寄りのアヒルは言い、アヒルらしい歩き方で水の中にもどっていきました。

とうとう、大きな卵が割れはじめました。「ピー！ ピー！」と、赤ちゃんアヒルが、卵から抜け出そうとしながら鳴きました。彼はとても大きくてみにくい子でした。お母さんはこの子を見ました。

「なんてみにくい子なんでしょう！」と彼女は叫びました。「他のどの子にも似ていないわ。この子はぜったいに七面鳥なんかじゃない！ とにかく、すぐにわかるでしょう！ この子を水の中に行かせなきゃ、背中を押してでもね！」

The Ugly Duckling

The weather was perfect the next day; the sun was shining on the green leaves and the blue water. The mother duck and her family walked down to the lake. "Quick! Quick!" cried she, and one after another dropped into the water. The water went over their heads for a moment. But soon they were all floating and moving about in the water with their legs; even the ugly gray duckling.

"No, it's no turkey!" said the mother duck. "See how nicely it uses its legs, and how straight it sits up in the water! It's my own young one! I suppose he's not so ugly after all. Rather pretty really, if you look closely. Quick! Quick! Come with me everyone into the great big world. I will present you to the duck yard. But keep close to me and watch out for the cat!"

And so they came into the duck yard. There was a loud noise. Two families were fighting over a fish head. Finally, the cat got it.

■sit up 姿勢正しくする　■after all 結局のところ　■closely 副 入念に　■watch out for ～に用心する　■fight over ～をめぐって言い争う

みにくいアヒルの子

　次の日、お天気は最高でした。太陽が緑の葉っぱと青い水の上で輝いていました。お母さんと子どもたちは、池まで歩きました。「早く！　早く！」とお母さんは叫び、アヒルの子どもたちは次から次へと水の中へ入っていきました。水はほんのつかの間、子どもたちの頭の上まできました。それでもすぐにみんな水の上に浮かび、脚で水をかいて動きまわりました。みにくい灰色のアヒルの子でさえ、そうしました。

　「この子は七面鳥じゃないわ！」とお母さんは言いました。「あの子は脚をとてもうまく使うし、水の中でとてもまっすぐにしていられるわ！あの子は私の子だわ！　よく見れば、あの子はそんなにみにくくないみたい。どちらかと言えばかわいいくらい、よく見ればね。早く！　早く！大きな世界へみんなでいっしょに行きましょう。アヒルの庭を見せてあげるわ。でも私のそばを離れないで、ネコにも気をつけるんですよ！」

　そうして、みんなはアヒルの庭へやって来ました。そこでは大きな音がしていました。二つの家族が魚の頭をめぐって争っていたのでした。とうとう、ネコがそれを取ってしまいました。

The Ugly Duckling

"Look, that is the way of the world!" said the mother duck. She too would have liked the fish head. "Use your legs," she said, "and look smart. Be nice to that old duck over there, for she is the most famous duck in the yard; her family comes from Spain; and see the red tie around her leg! That is a great honor; it means that they want to keep her, so men and animals must be kind to her. Quack! Quack! Don't turn your feet in! A well-brought-up duckling keeps his feet wide apart like father and mother! Look at me! Like so! And now stick out your neck and 'Quack!'"

As they did so, all the other ducks watching in the yard began to talk loudly. "Just look! Now we have all these new ones, too! There are already too many of us here! And oh, my! Look at that ugly gray duckling! Well, we don't need his kind around here!" Just then a duck flew at the big duckling and bit him in the neck.

"Leave him alone, will you!" said the mother. "He's not hurting you."

■the way of the world 世の習い　■nice 形行儀の良い　■tie 名ひも　■well-brought-up 形育ちの良い　■wide apart 大きく広げる　■stick out 突き出す　■bit 動bite（かみつく）の過去形　■leave ~ alone ～に手を出さない

みにくいアヒルの子

「あれを見なさい。世間とはああいうものよ！」お母さんは言いました。実は彼女も魚の頭が欲しかったのですけれども。「脚を使って」とお母さんは言いました。「そしてかしこそうに見せるのよ。あそこにいる年寄りのアヒルには行儀よくしなさい。あの方は、アヒルの庭で一番有名なんですから。あの家族はスペインから来たのです。脚に結んだ赤いひもをご覧なさい！　あれはとても名誉なことなんですよ。人間が彼女を飼っておきたいという意味なのです。だから人間も動物も、彼女には親切にしないといけないんですよ。ガー！　ガー！　脚を内側に入れるんじゃありません！　育ちのよいアヒルの子は、お父さんとお母さんと同じように、自分の両脚を広く開いたままにしておくものなんですから！　私をご覧なさい！　そうしているでしょう！　さあ、首を突き出して『ガー』と鳴きなさい！」

子どもたちがそうやって鳴くと、庭で見ていたほかのアヒルはみんな、声高に話し始めました。「ちょっと見てごらんよ！　新しい子たちが来たよ！　ここには今でも多すぎるくらいアヒルがいるのに！　それに、なんということだろう！　あのみにくい灰色の子を見てごらん！　とにかく、ああいう種類の子は、このあたりではいらないね！」ちょうどその時、一羽のアヒルが、その大きなみにくいアヒルの子に飛びかかり、首にかみつきました。

「この子を放っておいてちょうだい！」とお母さんは言いました。「この子はあなたを傷つけたりしていないのに」

The Ugly Duckling

"No, but he's so big and strange-looking!" said the duck who bit him, "so, we cannot accept him!"

"You have pretty children, mother!" said the old duck with the red tie around her leg. "They are all pretty except one, which hasn't turned out well at all! I wish you could make him over again!"

"Not possible, My Lady!" said the mother of the ducklings. "He isn't pretty, but he is well mannered and swims as well as the others. Even better, I must say! I think he will grow prettier, or perhaps smaller, in time. His problem is that he was in the egg too long!"

Then she straightened some of his feathers with her mouth. "Besides, he's a boy-duck," she said, "and so his beauty is not so important! I think he'll be strong enough to fight his way along!"

"The other ducklings are very nice," said the old duck. "Please make yourself at home; and if you find a fish head you may bring it to me."

■strange-looking 形 外観が奇妙な　■turn out well うまく収まる　■make over 作り直す　■well mannered 行儀の良い　■straighten 動 整える　■fight one's way along 自分の道を切り開く　■make oneself at home くつろぐ

みにくいアヒルの子

「そうだけど、コイツはすごく大きくて変わってるよ！」とみにくいアヒルの子をかんだアヒルは言いました。「だから、アイツを受け入れることはできないよ！」

「あなたの子どもたちはかわいいですよ、お母さん！」と、脚に赤いひもを結んだ年寄りのアヒルが言いました。「みんなかわいいね、一人を除けば。その子はぜんぜんかわいくないね！ その子をつくり直すことができたらいいんだがねえ！」

「それは無理ですわ、奥さま！」と、アヒルの子たちのお母さんは言いました。「この子はかわいいとは言えませんが、お行儀はよいし、他の子たちと同じくらいうまく泳げます。いえ、もっとうまいかもしれません！ この子はもう少ししたら、もっとかわいく、もしかしたらもっと小さくなるかもしれないですよ。この子の問題は、卵の中に長くいすぎたことなんです！」

そしてお母さんはくちばしで、みにくいアヒルの子の羽を整えてやりました。「それに、この子は男の子なんです」と彼女は言いました。「だから、かわいいかどうかなんて、重要なことじゃありません！ 私は、この子は自分の道を自分で切り開いていく強さが十分あると思いますわ！」

「他の子どもたちは、みんないい子だね」と年寄りのアヒルは言いました。「ここでゆっくりしておいき。それから、もし魚の頭を見つけたら、私に持ってきておくれ」

The Ugly Duckling

But the poor duckling who was the last born and looked so ugly had many problems. He was bitten, pushed and talked about by the other ducks and chickens. "He's too big!" they all cried. Everyone in the yard began to say mean, unkind things to him. Then they would laugh and laugh at him. The poor duckling didn't know what to do.

And so the first day was a very bad day for him. After that, things became even more difficult. The duckling was pushed about and bitten by them all. His own brothers and sisters kept saying, "If only the cat would eat you, you ugly thing!" while even his own mother said, "If only you were far, far away!" And the girl who fed the animals hit him with her foot.

Then he ran away from the yard. He ran past trees and plants causing little birds to fly into the air. "They fly away because I am so ugly." said the duckling. He closed his eyes and ran on. At last he came to a field where the wild ducks lived. There he lay all night long, tired and sad.

■bitten 動bite（かみつく）の過去分詞形　■talked about うわさを立てられる　■push about いじめる　■fed 動feed（〜に食物を与える）の過去形

みにくいアヒルの子

けれども、最後に生まれたみにくい、かわいそうなアヒルの子は、いろいろとたいへんな思いをしました。他のアヒルやニワトリからかまれたり、つきとばされたり、悪口を言われたりしました。「アイツは大きすぎるんだ！」とみんなが叫びました。庭にいるみんなが、意地悪な、ひどいことをみにくいアヒルの子に言い始めました。そして笑いものにしました。かわいそうなアヒルの子は、どうしたらいいかわかりませんでした。

そういうわけで、最初の日はみにくいアヒルの子にとってひどいものでした。でもその後、もっとひどいことになりました。みにくいアヒルの子はみんなにいじめられ、かまれました。自分の兄弟姉妹たちでさえ、こう言い続けました。「ネコがおまえのことを食べてしまえばいいのに、みにくいヤツめ！」お母さんでさえ、「おまえがどこか遠い、遠いところへ行ってくれたらいいのに！」と言いました。そして動物にエサをやる人間の女の子も、彼を蹴とばしました。

それから、みにくいアヒルの子は庭から逃げ出しました。木や植物があるその先へと走って行くと、小鳥たちは空に飛んでいきました。「鳥はぼくがこんなにみにくいから、飛んで行ってしまうんだ」とみにくいアヒルの子は言いました。彼は目をつぶってどんどん走りました。そして野生のカモが住んでいる草原へやってきました。みにくいアヒルの子は、疲れて悲しい思いで、そこに一晩中横になっていました。

The Ugly Duckling

In the morning the wild ducks saw their new neighbor. "What kind of a thing are you?" they asked. The duckling tried to say hello to them.

"You are quite ugly!" said the wild ducks; "but it doesn't matter to us as long as you do not marry into the family!"

Poor thing! He had no idea of marrying! It was enough for him just to lay in peace and quiet among the water plants.

There he lay for two whole days. Then there came two wild, rather young, boy-ducks who wanted to have a good time.

"Listen, friend!" they said; "you are so ugly that we quite like you. Won't you come play with us? Nearby, in another pond, are some really sweet and pretty young girl-ducks. As ugly as you are, they'll like you just the same!"

■not matter どうでもいい　■in peace 平和に　■water plant 水生植物

みにくいアヒルの子

　朝になり、野生のカモたちは新しい仲間を見ました。「君はどういう種類なの？」とカモは聞きました。アヒルの子は、カモにあいさつをしようとしました。
　「君は本当にみにくいね！」と野生のカモが言いました。「でも、君がぼくたちの家族と結婚しない限り、どうでもいいことだけどね！」

　かわいそうなアヒルの子！　彼は結婚なんて考えてもいませんでした！　水草の間に、ただ平和に静かに横たわっているだけで十分だったのでした。
　みにくいアヒルの子はそこにまるまる二日間横たわっていました。それから、二羽のやや若いオスの野生のカモが遊びにやって来ました。

　「ねえ、君！」とカモは言いました。「君はとってもみにくいから、君のことがすごく気に入ったよ。いっしょに遊ばないかい？　近くにあるほかの池には、とてもやさしくてかわいい若いカモの娘たちがいるよ。君ぐらいみにくいなら、同じく君のことを好きになってくれるさ！」

The Ugly Duckling

"Pop! Pop!" came a loud sound at that moment, and the two boy-ducks fell dead. The water turned blood-red. "Pop! Pop!" came more sounds from all around the pond. Many ducks were dying and the others were flying away. It was a hunting party. The hunters were firing their guns from behind plants and trees. Blue smoke was everywhere. The hunting dogs ran through the water, picking the ducks up in their mouths. The poor, ugly duckling was so afraid. He tried to put his head under his wing. Just then, a large dog stood right in front of the duckling. His mouth was open and his eyes were shining; his large, pointed teeth were touching the duckling—and suddenly! He turned and ran off.

"Oh, thank God!" thought the duckling. "I'm so ugly that even the dog won't bite me!"

And he laid very still among the water plants while the guns continued to fire away. Much later in the day, when all was quiet, the duckling lifted his head and looked around. Then he ran as fast as he could through fields and forests. But a strong wind was blowing against him, making him tired.

■fall dead 倒れて死ぬ ■blood-red 血のように赤い ■fly away 飛び去る ■hunting party 狩猟パーティー ■fire a gun 発砲する ■run off 走り去る ■Thank God! ああ、助かった！ ■fire away 発砲し続ける ■blow against〔風が〕(人)に向かって吹く

みにくいアヒルの子

「パン！ パン！」その瞬間、大きな音がしました。そして二羽の若いオスのカモは死んでしまいました。池の水は血で赤く染まりました。「パン！ パン！」池のまわりじゅうから、もっと音がしました。たくさんのカモが死んでいき、残りのカモは飛んでいってしまいました。それは狩猟のパーティーだったのです。狩人たちは、植物や木の陰から銃をうっていました。青い煙が充満していました。猟犬たちは水の中まで走ってきて、カモを口にくわえていました。かわいそうなみにくいアヒルの子は、とても怯えていました。彼は羽の下に頭を隠そうとしました。ちょうどその時、大きな犬が、みにくいアヒルの子のまん前に立っていました。犬の口は開き、目はギラギラと輝いていました。犬の大きくとがった歯がみにくいアヒルの子にまさに触れようとしたその時でした。それは突然のことでした！ 犬は向きを変え、走り去りました。

「ああ、助かった！」とみにくいアヒルの子は思いました。「ぼくがあんまりみにくいから、犬でさえぼくをかもうとしないんだ！」

そしてみにくいアヒルの子は、銃の玉が飛び交っている間、水生植物の間でじっとしていました。その日、時間がだいぶたち、すべてが静かになった時、みにくいアヒルの子は頭を持ち上げ、まわりを見渡しました。それからできるだけ速く、野原や森をぬけて走りました。けれども、強い向かい風のために、疲れてしまいました。

The Ugly Duckling

Finally, in the evening, he reached a little, old house. He was so tired and afraid. The house had an old, broken door that was half-open, so the duckling looked inside.

Here lived an old woman with her cat and her hen. The cat was called Sonny. He could raise his back and make cat sounds, "Purr! Purr!" The hen had fat little legs and was called Chicky-short-legs; She made hen sounds, "Cluck! Cluck!" She laid good eggs and the old woman loved her like a child.

The next morning they saw the ugly duckling sleeping outside the door. The cat purred and the hen clucked.

"I don't believe my eyes!" said the old woman looking at the duckling. But her eyes were not very good, so she thought the duckling was a fat duck which was lost. "Now maybe I can have duck eggs too. We must wait and see."

■hen 名めんどり　■laid 動lay（卵を産む）の過去形　■wait and see 成り行きを見守る

みにくいアヒルの子

　夜になってやっと、みにくいアヒルの子は、小さな古い家にたどり着きました。彼はとても疲れて、怯えていました。その家の古い壊れたドアが半分開いていたので、みにくいアヒルの子は中をのぞきこみました。

　そこにはおばあさんがネコとメンドリといっしょに住んでいました。ネコの名前はサニーといいました。彼は背中を持ち上げ、「ゴロ！　ゴロ！」とのどを鳴らすことができました。メンドリの脚は太くて短かったので、短足ニワトリちゃんと呼ばれていました。彼女はメンドリの「コッ！　コッ！」という声で鳴きました。メンドリはよい卵を産んだので、おばあさんは彼女を子どものようにかわいがっていました。

　次の朝、彼らは、ドアの外にみにくいアヒルの子が寝ているのを見つけました。ネコはのどをゴロゴロ鳴らし、メンドリはコッコッと鳴きました。

　「自分の目が信じられないよ！」と、おばあさんはアヒルの子を見ながら言いました。けれども、おばあさんの目はあまりよくなかったので、みにくいアヒルの子のことを、道に迷った太ったアヒルだと思いました。「これで、あたしにはアヒルの卵も手に入るかもしれない。みんなで待ってみなけりゃね」

The Ugly Duckling

So for three weeks the duckling was taken into the household; but he did not lay a single egg. The cat was the master in that house and the hen was the mistress. They always said: "We are the world!" because they thought that they were half the world. And the better half too! The duckling did not agree with them but the hen would not listen.

"Can you lay eggs?" she asked.

"No."

"Then be quiet!"

And the cat said. "Can you raise your back and purr?"

"No!"

"Then your opinions are not equal to ours." So the duckling sat unhappily in the corner. Then he thought of the fresh air and sunshine. Suddenly, he had such a strong desire to float upon the water that he told the hen of his feelings.

"What's wrong with you?" asked the hen. "You're out of your mind because you have nothing to do. Lay eggs or purr, and these strange ideas will go away!"

■be taken into the household 一家に入れられる　■mistress 图女主人　■unhappily 副不幸に　■in the corner 隅で　■what's wrong with 〜のどこが悪いのですか　■out of one's mind 頭がおかしい　■go away 消えうせる

みにくいアヒルの子

　それで三週間の間、みにくいアヒルの子はこの家にいました。けれども、一つの卵も産みませんでした。ネコはその家の主人で、メンドリは女主人でした。二人はいつもこう言っていました。「私たちが世界なんだ！」なぜなら、二人は自分のことを、世界の半分だと考えていたからです。しかもよい方の半分だと！　みにくいアヒルの子はそうは思いませんでしたが、メンドリは聞こうとしませんでした。

　「おまえは卵を産めるのかい？」とメンドリはたずねました。
　「いいえ」
　「それなら、静かにしておいで！」
　それからネコが言いました。「おまえは背中を高くしてのどをゴロゴロ鳴らせるかい？」
　「いいえ！」
　「それなら、おまえの意見は、我々のものと等しいとは言えない」それで、アヒルの子は隅の方に悲しそうに座りました。それから、新鮮な空気とお日さまの光のことを考えました。突然、アヒルの子は、水の上に浮かびたいと強く思ったので、そのことをメンドリに話しました。
　「おまえはどうかしちまったのかい？」とメンドリは聞きました。「おまえは何もすることがないから、頭がヘンになってしまったんだよ。卵を産むか、のどをゴロゴロ鳴らしてごらん。そしたらそんなとんでもない考えは吹っ飛んでいっちまうから！」

The Ugly Duckling

"But it's so nice to float upon the water!" said the duckling; "so nice to go under the water and down to the bottom!"

"Oh, you must be mad!" said the hen. "Ask the cat; he's the wisest person I know. If he likes floating on the water, I'll say no more. Ask the old woman; no one in the world is wiser than she. Do you think that she likes to float on or under the water?"

"You don't understand me!" said the duckling.

"If we don't understand you, I don't know who will! You will never be wiser than the three of us! Don't make a fool of yourself, child! You should thank heaven that we are so nice to you. Didn't we let you into a warm room with food to eat? You are an ugly sort of bird and being with you is not pleasant. Believe me. I'm telling you this as your friend, because it's true! You should learn to lay eggs or purr."

"I think I will go out into the wide world," said the duckling.

"Go right ahead!" said the hen.

■mad 形気が狂って　■say no more それ以上は言わない　■make a fool of oneself ばかなこと[まね]をする　■thank 動(人や物事を)ありがたいと思う　■sort 名種類　■go ahead さあどうぞ

みにくいアヒルの子

「でも、水の上に浮かんでいるのは、とっても気持ちがいいよ！」とアヒルの子は言いました。「水の下にもぐって底まで行ったりするのもね！」

「ああ、おまえは頭がヘンだよ！」とメンドリは言いました。「ネコに聞いてごらん。私が知っている中で一番かしこい人だから。もし彼が水の上に浮かんでいるのが好きだったら、あたしはもう何も言わないよ。おばあさんに聞いてごらん。この世のだれよりもかしこいんだから。おまえは、おばあさんが水の上に浮かんだり、水の下にいたりするのが好きだと思うかい？」

「あなたにはぼくのことはわからないんだ！」とアヒルの子は言いました。

「もしあたしたちがおまえのことをわからなければ、だれがわかると言うのさ！　おまえなんか、どうやったってあたしたち三人よりかしこくなることなんかできやしないんだからね！　ふざけるのもほどほどにおし、このちびっ子め！　あたしたちがこんなに親切にしてやってることを、おまえは天に感謝しなくちゃいけないよ。あたしたちがおまえをあったかい部屋へ入れてやって、食べさせてやったんじゃないかい？　おまえはみにくいたぐいの鳥だから、いっしょにいても楽しくないよ。本当なんだから。これはおまえの友達として言ってるんだよ。だってホントのことなんだから！　おまえは、卵を産むか、のどをゴロゴロ鳴らすか、どっちかできるようにならなくちゃ」

「ぼくは外の広い世界に行こうと思う」と、アヒルの子は言いました。

「さっさとお行き！」とメンドリは言いました。

The Ugly Duckling

So the duckling went. He floated on the water happily, but the other animals didn't talk to him because he was so ugly.

And now it was fall. The leaves of the forest grew yellow and brown, and the wind blew them all around. There was a cold look high in the sky. The clouds were heavy with cold rain and snow. On a fence stood a blackbird who cried "Ow! Ow!" because it was getting so cold. Oh, the poor duckling knew it wouldn't be easy.

One evening, during a beautiful sunset, a large group of lovely birds appeared from the nearby woods. The duckling had never seen anything so beautiful. They were bright white with long, pretty necks; they were swans. After making a strange cry, they spread their wings and flew up, up and up; away from the cold fields to warmer lands and lakes. They flew so high that the duckling could hardly see them. He turned around in the water and stuck out his neck to watch them.

■fence 名フェンス、柵　■blackbird 名クロウタドリ　■swan 名ハクチョウ　■spread one's wings 羽をいっぱいに広げる

みにくいアヒルの子

　それでアヒルの子は出ていきました。彼は幸せそうに水の上に浮かんでいましたが、他の動物たちは彼があんまりみにくいので、話しかけてきませんでした。

　そして、季節は秋になりました。森の木々の葉っぱは黄色や茶色になり、風がそれらをあちこちに吹き飛ばしていました。空の上の方は寒そうに見えました。雲は冷たい雨と雪で重くなっていました。柵の上ではクロウタドリが「オウ！　オウ！」と叫んでいました。とても寒くなってきていたからです。ああ、かわいそうなアヒルの子は、この先はたいへんになることがわかっていました。

　ある日の夕方、美しい日没の間に、近くの森からおおぜいの美しい鳥の一群が現れました。アヒルの子は、それほど美しいものは見たことがありませんでした。その鳥たちの色はまぶしいばかりに白く、長く美しい首をしていました。それは白鳥でした。不思議な声で鳴いたあと、白鳥は羽を広げ、高く、高く、高く飛んでいきました。冷たい野原から、もっと暖かい土地や湖があるところへと向かって行ったのです。白鳥はとても高いところを飛んでいたので、アヒルの子にはほとんど見えませんでした。アヒルの子は水の中で向きを変え、白鳥を見るために首を突き出しました。

The Ugly Duckling

🎧73　Oh! He could not forget those beautiful and happy birds. His heart was beating loudly, his eyes were wide. He did not know the name of the birds, or where they were flying. But he loved them. How joyful it would have been if they had asked him to go along! He knew he could never hope to be like them, though.

And the winter grew colder and colder. The duckling had to keep swimming to stop the water from becoming ice. But every night more water turned to ice. Finally the poor duckling was too tired to swim anymore. He lay quite still until he became stuck in the ice.

Early the next morning a farmer passed that way. He saw the duckling, went out to it, and broke the ice with his wooden shoe. He brought the bird home to his wife, and the duckling was saved.

The children wanted to play with him, but the duckling was afraid. He flew around the room and right into the milkcan. Then he flew into the butter dish and the grain. Soon, there was milk and butter and grain everywhere.

■beat 動鼓動する　■How ~ it would have been if ... もし…だったとしたらどんなにか~だっただろう　■go along（人）について行く　■go out to ～まで足を延ばす　■milkcan 名牛乳缶　■butter dish バター皿　■grain 名穀物

みにくいアヒルの子

　ああ！　アヒルの子は、あの美しく、幸せそうな鳥たちを忘れることはできませんでした。アヒルの子の心臓はドキドキし、目は大きく見開かれていました。その鳥たちの名前を知らなかったし、どこへ飛んで行くのかも知りませんでした。でも、彼らを愛しました。もしいっしょに行こうと誘ってくれたら、どんなにうれしかったことでしょう！　けれども、アヒルの子は、白鳥のようになりたいと望むことはけっしてできないことを知っていました。

　そして、冬の寒さはもっともっと厳しくなってきました。アヒルの子は、水が凍ってしまわないように、泳ぎ続けなければなりませんでした。けれども、毎晩、さらに多くの水が氷になっていきました。ついに、かわいそうなアヒルの子は疲れてしまい、もう泳げなくなりました。彼は動かずにじっと横になり、ついには氷にはまってしまいました。

　次の日の朝早く、一人の農夫がそこを通りかかりました。農夫はアヒルの子を見つけ、彼のところまで行き、木ぐつで氷を割りました。農夫はアヒルの子を、奥さんのいる家へ連れて帰ったので、アヒルの子の命は助かりました。

　農夫の子どもたちはアヒルの子と遊びたかったのですが、アヒルの子は怖がりました。彼は部屋の中を飛びまわり、牛乳缶の中に入ってしまいました。それからバター皿と穀物の中に飛び込みました。やがて、牛乳とバターと穀物がそこら中に散らばりました。

The Ugly Duckling

　　The woman shouted and tried to hit the duckling with a pot; the children, laughing and falling, tried to catch it. The door was open though, and out it flew into the freshly fallen snow. He hurried into some plants and lay there so sadly.

　　The poor duckling had such an unhappy and difficult winter that year. Too sad to talk about, really. He was lying in a small pond among plants when the sun began to shine warmly; the other birds began to sing because it was springtime again.

　　One day the duckling spread its wings; they were stronger than before, and he began to fly easily. Before he knew where he was going he had arrived in a beautiful, large garden. The tree leaves were a fresh green and the bright flowers smelled lovely. In the middle of this beautiful place was a pond. Suddenly, right in front of him, there appeared three beautiful white swans. They made a rushing sound with their wings and floated on the water. The duckling remembered seeing these lovely birds and felt a strange sadness.

■warmly 副温かく　■springtime 名春　■before someone knew 知らない間に

みにくいアヒルの子

　奥さんは叫び、アヒルの子を鍋で叩こうとしました。子どもたちは笑ったり転んだりしながら、アヒルの子を捕まえようとしました。けれどもドアが開いていたので、アヒルの子は降ったばかりの雪の中に飛び出していきました。彼は急いで植物の陰に行き、とても悲しい思いで、そこに横たわっていました。
　かわいそうなアヒルの子は、その年、とても不幸でたいへんな冬を過ごしました。本当に、あまりにも悲しいお話なので、そのことについては話さないでおきましょう。アヒルの子は、お日さまが暖かく照り始めた時、小さな池の植物の間に横たわっていました。他の鳥たちは、また春がやってきたので、歌い始めました。
　ある日、アヒルの子は羽を広げました。羽は前よりも強くなっていたので、彼は簡単に飛び始めました。自分がどこへ向かっているのかもわからないうちに、アヒルの子は美しい、大きな庭園に着きました。木の葉は新鮮な緑色をしており、明るい色の花はすばらしい香りでした。この美しい場所のまん中は、池でした。突然、彼のまん前に、三羽の美しい白鳥が現れました。白鳥は羽で激しい音を立てて、水の上に浮かびました。アヒルの子はこの美しい鳥たちを見たことがあるのを思い出し、不思議な悲しさを感じました。

The Ugly Duckling

"I will fly towards these fine birds! They will bite me because I am so ugly and dare to come near them; but I don't care anymore. It is better they kill me than to continue living as I have. No, I couldn't stand another winter!"

So he flew out into the pond, and swam towards the swans. When they saw the duckling they rushed towards him quickly. "Kill me and end my sadness!" cried the poor duck. He lowered his head and waited for death. But what did he see in the clear water? Himself? Was it possible? He was no longer a strange, large, dark-gray and very ugly bird; he too was a swan!

It doesn't matter at all about being born in a duck-yard if one comes from a swan's egg. The large swans now swam around and around him; they touched him with their mouths and were very friendly.

■stand 動 〜を我慢する

みにくいアヒルの子

「ぼくはあのすばらしい鳥たちの方へ飛んでいくだろう！　ぼくはとてもみにくいので、彼らはぼくにかみつき、そばに来られないようにするだろう。でもぼくはもう気にしない。今までのように生きていかなきゃならないんだったら、彼らに殺される方がましだ。いやだ、もう一度冬を越すなんて、もう耐えられない！」

それからアヒルの子は池の中へ飛んで行き、白鳥の方へ泳いでいきました。白鳥はアヒルの子を見ると、すぐに彼の方へやって来ました。「ぼくを殺して、この悲しみを終わりにしてください！」と、かわいそうなアヒルの子は叫びました。彼は頭を下げ、死を待ちました。ところが、彼は澄み切った水の中に、何を見たでしょうか？　これが自分？　そんなことがあるでしょうか？　アヒルの子はもはや不格好な、大きな、濃い灰色のとてもみにくい鳥ではありませんでした。自分も白鳥だったのです！

もし白鳥の卵から生まれたのなら、アヒルの庭で生まれたことなど問題ではありません。大きな白鳥たちは、今はアヒルの子のまわりを泳ぎまわっていました。白鳥は口で彼に触り、そして、とても親切でした。

The Ugly Duckling

Some little children came running into the garden; they threw corn and bread on the water, and the smallest of them said: "There's a new one!" The other children also shouted, "Yes! A new one has come!" They jumped up and down and ran to get their mother and father. More bread and cakes were thrown into the water, and they all said: "The new one is the prettiest! It is so young and lovely!" And the old swans lowered their heads before him.

He felt so shy that he stuck his head under his wings and didn't know what to do. He was almost too happy, but not proud; for a good heart is never proud. He thought of how he had been so completely disliked; and now all said he was the loveliest of lovely birds. And the flowers turned towards him and the sun shone nice and warm. Then the swan spread out his feathers, raised his fine neck, and cried from the bottom of his heart: "I never dreamed of such happiness when I was an ugly duckling!"

■bread 名パン ■thrown 動throw（投げる）の過去分詞形 ■shy 形内気な ■proud 形高慢な ■completely 副完全に ■be disliked 嫌われる

みにくいアヒルの子

　小さな子どもたちが、庭の中に駆け込んで来ました。その子たちは、トウモロコシやパンを水の上に投げました。すると、一番小さな子がこう言いました。「新しいのがいるよ！」ほかの子どもたちもみんな叫びました。「本当だ！　新しいのが来た！」子どもたちは飛び跳ね、お父さんとお母さんを呼びに走っていきました。もっとたくさんパンとケーキが水の中に投げ込まれ、みんなこう言いました。「新しいのが一番きれいだ！　あの鳥はとても若くてきれいだな！」　年寄りの白鳥たちは、アヒルの子の前で頭を下げました。

　アヒルの子はとても恥ずかしがり屋だったので、頭を羽の下に突っ込み、どうしたらいいのかわかりませんでした。ほとんど幸せすぎるくらいでしたが、彼は高慢ではありませんでした。よい心の持ち主は、けっして高慢な気持ちをもったりしないからです。彼は自分が今までどんなにひどく嫌われてきたかを考えました。そして今は、みんなが自分のことを、美しい鳥の中でも一番美しいと言ってくれました。花々は彼の方にふり向き、お日さまはすてきに輝き、暖かいのでした。それから白鳥は羽を広げ、美しい首を上げ、心の底からこう叫びました。「ぼくがみにくいアヒルの子だった時には、自分にこんな幸せがくるなんて、夢にも思わなかったよ！」

覚えておきたい英語表現

> **Please make yourself at home.** （p. 148, 下から2行目）
> （我が家にいるかのように）ゆっくりしてください。

【解説】makeの基本的意味に「あるものを、ある状態にする」という意味があります。Your smiles make me happy. なら、「あなたのほほえみが、私を幸せにしてくれる」という意味になります。今回の例文は、「あなた自身を自分の家にいるかのように、くつろいだ状態にしてください」という意味を表します。日常会話でもよく使われる表現です。

【例文】　Please make yourself relaxed with this music.
　　　　　（この音楽を聴いて、リラックスしてください）

　　　　　This medicine will make you feel better.
　　　　　（この薬を飲むと、気分がよくなるでしょう）

　　　　　Just one glass of beer made me happy.
　　　　　（たった1杯のビールで、私は気分がよくなった）

> Won't you come play with us?（p. 152, 下から3行目）
> ぼくたちといっしょに遊ばないか？

【解説】「相手の人からYes.の答えを期待するときには、否定の疑問文で話しかけてみるといいでしょう。たとえばAren't you hungry?（おなか空いていない？空いているよね）という感じです。

【例文】　Don't you think the President is wrong?
　　　　（大統領の言っていること間違っていると思わないかい？）

　　　　Aren't there any good Italian restaurant near here?
　　　　（この近くにおいしいイタリアンレストラン、ありませんか？）

　　　　Haven't you ever been to Okinawa?
　　　　（沖縄に行ったこと、ありませんでしたか？）

　　　　Didn't you say you love me?
　　　　（僕のこと、愛しているって、言わなかった？）

E-CATとは…
英語が話せるようになるための
テストです。インターネット
ベースで、30分であなたの発
話力をチェックします。

www.ecatexam.com

● iTEP®とは…
世界各国の企業、政府機関、アメリカの大学
300校以上が、英語能力判定テストとして採用。
オンラインによる90分のテストで文法、リー
ディング、リスニング、ライティング、スピー
キングの5技能をスコア化。iTEP®は、留学、就
職、海外赴任などに必要な、世界に通用する英
語力を総合的に評価する画期的なテストです。

www.itepexamjapan.com

[IBC対訳ライブラリー]
英語で読むアンデルセン名作選

2019年2月4日　第1刷発行

原 著 者　ハンス・クリスチャン・アンデルセン
翻　　訳　佐　藤　和　枝
英語解説　谷　口　幸　夫

発行者　浦　　晋　亮

発行所　IBCパブリッシング株式会社
　　　　〒162-0804 東京都新宿区中里町29番3号 菱秀神楽坂ビル9F
　　　　Tel. 03-3513-4511　Fax. 03-3513-4512
　　　　www.ibcpub.co.jp

印刷所　株式会社シナノパブリッシングプレス
CDプレス　株式会社ケーエヌコーポレーションジャパン

© IBC Publishing, Inc. 2019

Printed in Japan

落丁本・乱丁本は、小社宛にお送りください。送料小社負担にてお取り替えいたします。
本書の無断複写（コピー）は著作権法上での例外を除き禁じられています。

ISBN978-4-7946-0573-3